A Student's Reference Grammar of Modern Formal Indonesian

R. Ross Macdonald

Soenjono Darjowidjojo

Georgetown University Press
Washington, D.C. 20007
1967

The research reported herein was performed pursuant to a contract with the Office of Education, United States Department of Health, Education, and Welfare. Contractors undertaking such projects under Government sponsorship are encouraged to express freely their professional judgment in the conduct of the project. Points of view or opinions stated do not, therefore, necessarily represent official Office of Education position or policy.

The cover design
shows Indonesian pierced-leather puppets
as they appear in shadow plays.

F O R E W O R D

This short book bears a long title: A Student's Reference Grammar of Modern Formal Indonesian. The reason for the shortness of the book is that a full description of the many intricacies of modern Indonesian still requires a great deal of research. As it now stands, however, this grammar is half as long again as was originally anticipated, and fascinating paths are still opening before the authors' eyes.

This grammar is a description of formal Indonesian in that it is based on published texts rather than on colloquial material. Some of the texts were delivered as political speeches; some are legal documents such as the Constitution and the Agrarian Laws; some are textbooks intended for use in schools; some are translations of books from other languages, generally through the medium of English; and a few are novelettes and stories. In some of these last, it is true, there is material of highly colloquial nature, but illustrative examples were culled from the colloquial material only when they were not easily found in more formal texts. In some cases, especially in the earlier chapters of the grammar, brief examples were created to illustrate points, but, on the whole, a conscientious attempt was made to base the description on actual occurrences in formally published texts.

The original intent was that each example cited should be identified as to its author and its place of origin. This intention was not carried out for two chief reasons. First, it was difficult to arrange an indexing system which would not clutter the text with reference numbers or with other impedimenta. Since many of the sources used are probably no longer available in comparable formats even in Indonesia, and since many are of considerable length, it would have been no easy task to devise a compact system which would still allow the reader quick access to the precise source of any specific quotation. Second, it seems unlikely that the greater percentage of the users of the grammar would be interested in ascertaining the exact source of every last example. For these reasons, the source of the examples has not been noted in the text. If anyone should be interested in the source of any specific example or set of examples, the author will be happy to supply the references upon application.

The Indonesian described here is called modern Indonesian because all of the texts on which the description is based were produced between 1945 and 1966.

This grammar is intended primarily for the general student of the Indonesian language, and only secondarily for the professional linguist. The description scrupulously endeavors to avoid both linguistic jargon (beyond terms reasonably well defined in general dictionaries) and too slavish a devotion to one particular grammatical model. The hope is that the description will be accessible to the general reader without being unpalatable to the linguist; a further hope is that the general reader will find it useful in his study of the Indonesian language, while the linguist will find it useful as a point of departure for more intensive studies of the Indonesian language.

It is customary to provide an index so that the user may find specific items conveniently and quickly. After experimentation, however, it has been decided that a merely alphabetic listing of terms would be less useful than a finely detailed table of contents. At first, it may require slightly more time to locate items by this means, but, as the overall structure of the book becomes more apparent, it will be easier to find specific areas of the discussion and those other areas which relate directly to them.

This grammar is the outcome of a long and fruitful association between its two authors. Unfortunately, Mr. Soenjono had to return to Indonesia before the text was in its final form. The basic description had already been elaborated, but the selection of specific examples to illustrate certain points had not yet been completed. I will therefore take entirely upon myself the responsibility for such errors or misstatements as occur.

It is with an almost insuperable reluctance that I deliver this text to the printer, because I am completely aware that many sections need improvement, many questions need more detailed discussion, and many more questions yet simply need discussion. But if I keep the text until I am entirely satisfied with it, it may never be published at all. And so I am sending the book out in the hope that the various discussions and criticisms of the present edition will lead to the production of a longer, stronger, and more complete second edition at a later date.

R. Ross Macdonald
November 1967

C O N T E N T S

INTRODUCTION

The language of Indonesia is Bahasa Indonesia. It is based on Malay (Bahasa Melaju), one of the more than two hundred local languages spoken in the East Indies. Malay, which is spoken in the Malay Peninsula, and, with minor differences, in East Central Sumatra, was the language first encountered by the cultural influences emanating from the mainland of Asia, and so it became, to some extent, a vehicle for the spread of these influences. It was the language of the medieval empire of Sriwidjaja, which had its center in Sumatra. and which controlled different other parts of the archipelago at different times. It was the language of the energetic Malay traders, and consequently came to be used also by the Arabs and the Portuguese as a trading language. For all of these reasons it became widely current throughout the islands as a means of intercommunication between speakers of different local languages.

When the Dutch entered the islands, they too used Malay extensively for commercial purposes.

While the Malay language was officially recognized, along with Dutch, for use in the People's Assembly or Council of the Colonial Regime, it was, in actual fact, hardly ever heard, and Dutch was established as the "language of advantage."

In 1928, the delegates to the Youth Congress which met in Djakarta adopted a resolution that for them there was one nation and one fatherland --Indonesia, and that there should be one language --Bahasa Indonesia. This is probably the first time that Bahasa Melaju was called Bahasa Indonesia.

Then the Second World War came. After the Japanese occupied the islands in 1942, they discontinued the use of Dutch. It was not practical to teach everyone Japanese in a short time, however. Under these circumstances, Bahasa Melaju, or Bahasa Indonesia, came into still wider use, and was fostered by the Japanese for administrative purposes.

Bahasa Indonesia was declared to be the national language in 1945, when Indonesia became an independent country under the Dutch crown, and again in 1949, when Indonesia became completely independent. Thus, Bahasa Melaju changed from, in 1940, a trading language still used largely in the bazaars and market places to, in 1950, the official language for all purposes of a country of well over sixty million people, a country growing rapidly and planning rapid modernization and development.

Soon the developments in the British colonies in the East Indies produced another independent nation, Malaysia, and Bahasa Melaju became one of the official languages of this new nation also.

Thus Bahasa Indonesia and Bahasa Melaju, essentially one and the same language, have become of marked importance in the area of South-East Asia.

There have been many changes in Bahasa Indonesia as a result of its historical development. Words have been freely borrowed from other languages and only partly assimilated, in many cases, to the Indonesian patterns of structure.

Sanskrit, because of the spread of Hindu culture, Arabic, because of the influence of the Moslem religion, and the Graeco-Latin vocabulary of Western Europe, because of the surge of technical development during this century, have especially contributed resources to Bahasa Indonesia-Melaju. Attempts have been made to create Indonesian vocabulary where a word was lacking, or where a borrowed word did not follow the Indonesian pattern. Words have also been freely adopted from the local languages, such as Javanese and Minangkabau. The demand for a comprehensive and flexible vocabulary can only increase as trade, technology and the interchange of information continue to expand.

Until some years ago (c. 1960), Bahasa Indonesia was the medium of instruction in the schools of Indonesia from the fourth grade on. In the first three grades, the pupils were taught in their local language and studied Bahasa Indonesia as one of the school subjects. Recently, the government has begun more and more to introduce Indonesian in the first grade as a medium of instruction. In some schools, even in Central and East Java, Indonesian is used from the beginning in the classroom. The interplay between Bahasa Indonesia on one hand, and the local language on the other, is becoming a matter of "academic" versus "home" environment.

But for most of the contemporary population Bahasa Indonesia is still a second language. The speakers of Javanese Sundanese, Balinese, Batak, Buginese and Timorese, to name but a few, constantly introduce features of their own language into the Indonesian they speak. Since the Javanese are numerically superior to the other groups, Javanisms are most frequently encountered; since Djakarta is the administrative center of the country, and the source of most radio broadcasts and newspaper reports, the Djakarta dialect is also an important influence.

The newspapers, which obtain their overseas news dispatches largely from English-speaking sources, are sometimes strongly influenced by English terms of expression even after the material has been translated into Indonesian.

Bahasa Indonesia today is probably changing as quickly as any language can. This adds very considerably to the difficulty of writing a description of the language. While every attempt has been made to describe here those aspects of the language which are most widely accepted, this book is proffered with the keen awareness that not every Indonesian will subscribe to every statement in it today, and that probably many fewer will do so twenty years from now.

P H O N O L O G Y

1.0 Phonemes

1.0.1 A human being is capable of producing a very large number of different vocal sounds. Each language treats some of the differences between these sounds as distinctive, using these particular differences as points of contrast to distinguish the forms of that language from each other. The other differences are treated as non-distinctive. Similar sounds which fall together because they are not recognized as distinct from each other in that particular language form a class which is known as a phoneme of that language. The members of each phoneme in a language contrast with the members of each other phoneme. The sounds which are grouped together in any one phoneme do not contrast with each other, then, but any sound of one phoneme contrasts with any sound of another phoneme. The phonemes of a language are thus the points of contrast in the phonological organization of the language.

As has been indicated, there may be perceptibly different sounds which are members of the same phoneme in a particular language. Because these subgroups of sounds occur in different environments or are freely interchangeable, however, they are never in direct contrast with each other. These subgroups are the allophones of the phoneme.

Each language has its own distinctive phonemic system; moreover, different dialects and formal levels of a language may have differing, though generally similar, phonemic systems.

1.0.2 There are differences among the phonemic systems used by various speakers of Indonesian both in the number and distribution of the phonemes and in the allophonic patterning. Since this grammar describes formal Indonesian, which is strongly influenced by the orthography, the phonemic system described here is that reflected by the orthography. Variations in pronunciation which are reflected in the orthography are also discussed, so that variant spellings may be correlated and recognized as one pattern.

1.0.3 Indonesian (as described here) has 30 phonemes, which will be symbolized as follows:

	Labial	Dental	Palatal	Velar	Glottal
Stops	/p/	/t/	/c̃/	/k/	/q/
	/b/	/d/	/j̃/	/g/	
Spirants	/f/	/s/	/s̃/	/x/	/h/
	/v/	/z/			
Nasals	/m/	/n/	/ñ/	/n̜/	
Trill		/r/			
Lateral		/l/			

	Front	Central	Back
Semivowels	/y/		/w/
Vowels, High	/i/		/u/
Medium	/e/	/ë/	/o/
Low		/a/	

1. 1 Stop Consonants

1.1.1.1 /p/

There is a bilabial unvoiced oral stop phoneme /p/. It occurs initially and finally in the syllable. When final before a pause or another consonant, it is usually unreleased. It resembles the sound in English <u>spin</u>, never the aspirated sound in the English <u>pin</u>.

It is represented in the writing system by the letter <u>P</u>, <u>p</u>. See also /b/, (Section 1.1.1.2).

/pena/	pena	'pen'
/harap/	harap	'hope'

1.1.1.2 /b/

There is a bilabial voiced oral stop phoneme /b/. It occurs initially in the syllable.

It resembles the sound in English <u>bin</u>, but is completely voiced.

It is represented in the writing system by the letter <u>B</u>, <u>b</u>.

/buku/	buku	'book'
/babu/	babu	'maid-servant'

The letter <u>b</u> at the end of a word (always a loan-word from other languages) represents the phoneme /p/, since the phoneme /b/ does not occur in this position.

/sëbap/	sebab	'reason'

1.1.2.1 /t/

There is an apico-dental or apico-alveolar unvoiced oral stop phoneme /t/. It occurs initially and finally in the syllable. When final before a pause or another consonant, it is usually unreleased.

It resembles the sound in English *stick*, never the aspirated sound in English *tick*.

It is represented in the writing system by the letter *T*, *t*. See also /d/ (1.1.2.2) and /c̃/ (1.1.3.1).

/tutup/	tutup	'close'
/amat/	amat	'very'

1.1.2.2 /d/

There is an apico-dental or apico-alveolar voiced oral stop phoneme /d/. It occurs initially in the syllable.

It resembles the sound in English *did*, but is completely voiced.

It is represented in the writing system by the letter *D*, *d*. See also /j̃/ (1.1.3.2).

/diri/	diri	'self'
/dada/	dada	'chest'

The letter *d* at the end of a word (always a loan-word from another language) represents the phoneme /t/, since the phoneme /d/ does not occur in this position.

/murit/	murid	'student'

1.1.3 The affricated stops described here, along with the spirant and nasal of the same order (s̃, ñ), are interpretable as unit phonemes. They may also be interpreted as clusters consisting of the apico-dental series followed by the semivowel /y/; the former alternative is chosen here. The orthography of Indonesian represents these sounds by clusters (tj, dj, sj, nj), because the Dutch orthographic conventions for similar sounds in Dutch were adopted for transcribing these sounds. The orthography of Malay represents them variously as ch, j, sh, ny because these writings conform to the English orthographic conventions.

1.1.3.1 /c̃/

There is a lamino-dental (or lamino-alveolar) unvoiced affricated oral stop phoneme /c̃/. It occurs initially in the syllable.

It resembles the sound in English cheese, not the sound in the English choose, in which the tongue is usually too far back in the mouth.

It is represented in the writing system by the digraph Tj, tj (Indonesian) or Ch, ch (Malay).

/c̃uc̃i/	tjutji (I) chuchi (M)	'launder'
/c̃ic̃aq/	tjitjak (I) chichak (M)	'house-lizard'

(Occasionally, items ending with tj are found in Indonesian dictionaries. Such words are borrowed from Arabic, and are so strongly felt to be Arabic that Indonesian speakers do not use them as Indonesian, but as purely foreign words.)

1.1.3.2 /j̃/

There is a lamino-dental (or lamino-alveolar) voiced affricated oral stop phoneme /j̃/. It occurs initially in the syllable.

It resembles the sound in the English jeep, with the tongue well forward in the mouth.

It is represented in the writing system by the digraph Dj, dj (Indonesian) and by the letter J, j (Malay).

/ǰadi/	djadi (I) jadi (M)	'become'
/ǰumaqat/	Djuma'at (I) Juma'at (M)	'Friday'

(The occasional words listed in the dictionary as ending in <u>dj</u> are felt to be foreign and non-Indonesian.)

1.1.4.1 /k/

There is a dorso-velar unvoiced oral stop phoneme /k/. It occurs initially in the syllable; it sometimes occurs finally in loan-words with certain speakers: /listërik/, 'electricity'. When it occurs finally before a pause or another consonant, it is usually unreleased.

It resembles the sound in the English <u>skin</u> or <u>scan</u>, never the aspirated sound in English <u>kin</u> or <u>can</u>.

It is represented in the writing system by the letter <u>K</u>, <u>k</u>; this letter has other values also. See /g/ (1.1.4.2) and /q/ (1.1.5).

/kuku/	kuku	'(finger)nail'
/kaki/	kaki	'foot'
/listërik/	listrik	'electricity'

1.1.4.2 /g/

There is a dorso-velar voiced oral stop phoneme /g/. It occurs initially in the syllable.

It resembles the sound in the English <u>get</u> or <u>go</u>, but is completely voiced.

It is represented in the writing system by the letter <u>G</u>, <u>g</u>. This letter is also used in the digraph <u>ng</u>. See /ŋ/ (1.3.4).

/gigi/	gigi	'tooth'
/ganti/	ganti	'replace'

The letter g at the end of a word (a loan-word) represents the phoneme /k/, since the phoneme /g/ does not occur in this position; the phoneme /k/ is unusual in this position also, except in loan-words.

/bëduk/	bedug	'drum (in a mosque)'

1.1.5 /q/

The various languages of the East Indies differ considerably in the distribution of the glottal stop, and various speakers are apt to bring the patterns of their regional language into Indonesian. Thus the Sundanese and Djakartanese may close syllables with a glottal stop which in cognate words in standard Indonesian are open. It is not to be expected that this will affect the spelling in any way, however, unless the author is deliberately trying to give the effect of a Sundanese speaking Indonesian.

There is a glottal stop phoneme /q/. It occurs both initially and finally in the syllable.

When /q/ is final in the syllable, it is strongly articulated.

/pendeq/	pendek	'short'
/raqyat/	rakjat	'people'

With some speakers it may be replaced in this position by the phoneme /k/. This is due in part to carry-over from the speaker's local language, and in part to the spelling conventions for this phoneme. There is a greater tendency for /k/ to replace /q/ when a suffix follows (/-an, -i, -kan/).

When /q/ is initial in the syllable, it is weakly articulated.

/qapi/	api	'fire'
/qibu/	ibu	'mother'

If, however, there is an immediately preceding vowel phoneme which is the same as the immediately following vowel phoneme it is again strongly articulated.

/maqaf/	ma'af or maaf	'pardon'

There is no consistently used English sound which resembles this Indonesian sound. When, instead of saying no, an English speaker says uh-uh, a glottal stop occurs between the two parts of this expression.

This phoneme /q/ is represented in the orthography in three ways:

a) When final in the syllable, it is represented by K, k.

/pendeq/	pendek	'short'
/raqyat/	rakjat	'people'

b) When initial in the syllable, it is not represented by any letter.

/qapi/	api	'fire'
/qibu/	ibu	'mother'

c) In certain loan-words, particularly from the Arabic, it is infrequently represented by an apostrophe, especially in the Malay orthography, but also by the convention described in a) or b).

/maqaf/	ma'af or maaf	'pardon'
/raqyat/	ra'jat or rakjat (I) ra'yat or rakyat (M)	'people'

1.2 Spirant Consonants

1.2.1.1 /f/

There is a labio-dental unvoiced fricative phoneme /f/. It occurs initially and finally.

It is represented in the writing system by the letter F, f.

It resembles the sound in English fat.

This phoneme occurs only in borrowings from other languages. All words in which this phoneme occurs have an alternate form in which the phoneme /p/ occurs.

/fikir/ or /pikir/ 'thought'

The phoneme /f/ occurs most frequently in words of Arabic origin, and so is most frequently used in the more strongly Moslem areas, and particularly by those people who are trained in the reading of the Koran. Much less frequently does it occur in words borrowed from Western European languages.

/fonim/ or /ponim/ 'phoneme'

In such cases the alternant with /p/ is more frequent.

/konpërensi/ or /konfërensi/ 'conference'

Although any /f/ may alternate with /p/, not every /p/ may alternate with /f/. Those words in which /f/ is pronounced are usually written with the letter F, f, and are listed in this way in dictionaries; those words or alternants in which /p/ is pronounced are, naturally, written with the letter P, p.

/fikir/	fikir	'thought'
/fonim/	fonim	'phoneme'
/konfërensi/	konferensi	'conference'
/pikir/	pikir	'thought'
/ponim/	ponim	'phoneme'
/konpërensi/	konperensi	'conference'

1.2.1.2 /v/

There is a bilabial or labio-dental voiced fricative phoneme /v/. It occurs initially in the syllable.

This phoneme occurs only marginally in borrowings from other languages, especially from European languages. The vast majority of speakers does not use this phoneme, but uses an alternate form with the phoneme /f/ or /p/.

When it does occur, it resembles the sound in English _va_t.

/fakansi/ or /pakansi/ or /vakansi/ 'vacation'

This phoneme is represented in the writing system by the letter _V_, _v_ in Indonesian; it is scarcely to be found in Malay.

/vakansi/	vakansi	'vacation'
/vak/	vak	'subject (of study)'

It is usual to write _V_, _v_ even when the pronunciation is /f/.

/fakansi/	vakansi
/fak/	vak

1.2.2.1 /s/

There is an apico-dental or apico-alveolar voiceless groove spirant /s/. It occurs both initially and finally in the syllable.

It resembles the sound in English sat.

It is represented in the writing system by the letters S, s.

/sisir/	sisir	'comb, hand (of bananas)'
/halus/	halus	'fine, delicate'

1.2.2.2 /z/

There is an apico-dental or apico-alveolar voiced groove spirant /z/. It occurs initially in the syllable. Any word in which this phoneme occurs will have alternate forms in which the phoneme /z/ is replaced either by the cluster /dz/ (less usually) or by the phoneme /ǰ/ (more usually). Such words are borrowed from Arabic; the pronunciation /dz/ is likely to be heard only in strongly Moslem communities. The pronunciation /ǰ/ is in general use.

/djaman/ or /dzaman/ or /zaman/ 'time'

This phoneme, when it occurs, resembles the sound in English zoo, but is completely voiced.

This phoneme is represented in the writing system by the letter Z, z. Words which are written with this letter may also occur with the digraphs dz or dj.

/zaman/	zaman	'time, era'

1.2.3 /š/

There is a lamino-dental or lamino-alveolar voiceless slit spirant /š/. It occurs initially in the syllable. It is a marginal phoneme, however, occurring in words of foreign origin; many speakers use the phoneme /s/ instead.

/mašarakat/ or /masarakat/	'society'
/šarat/ or /sarat/	'condition'
/šah/ or /sah/	'shah'

When it occurs, /š/ resembles the sound in English _issue_, with the tongue well forward in the mouth.

It is represented in the orthography by the digraph _Sj_, _sj_ (Indonesian) or _Sh_, _sh_ (Malay).

/mašarakat/	masjarakat (I) masharakat (M)	'society'
/šarat/	sjarat (I) sharat (M)	'condition'
/šah/	sjah (I) shah (M)	'ruler, shah'

1.2.4 /x/

There is a dorso-velar voiceless fricative phoneme /x/. It occurs initially in the syllable, but only in borrowed words, chiefly of Arabic origin. Many words in which this phoneme occurs have an alternate form in which the phoneme /k/ occurs instead.

/xabar/ or /kabar/	'news'
/xawatir/ or /kuatir/ or /kawatir/	'anxious'

(But /xas/ 'obvious' contrasts with /kas/ 'treasury' and with /has/ 'filet', and so does not customarily show this alternation.)

When it occurs, /x/ resembles the sound at the end of Scottish _loch_, or German _ach_.

This phoneme is represented in the writing system by the digraph _Ch_, _ch_ in Indonesian and the digraph _Kh_, _kh_ in Malay; words which are written with these digraphs are also written _K_, _k_ if the alternation of the phonemes /x/ and /k/ occurs.

/xabar/	chabar (I) khabar (M)	'news'
/xawatir/	chawatir (I) khuatir (M)	'anxious'
/xas/	chas (I) khas (M)	'obvious'

1.2.5 /h/

There is a voiceless glottal spirant phoneme /h/. This phoneme includes the voiceless onglide to a following vowel and the voiceless offglide from a preceding vowel. It occurs both initially and finally in the syllable. It is a strong unvoicing when final in the syllable. It is a somewhat weaker unvoicing when it is initial in the syllable, and with some speakers in certain cases, particularly when the surrounding vowels are different in quality, may disappear entirely.

/habis/ or /abis/	'finished'
/sudah/	'already'
/mahal/	'expensive'
/lahir/	'bear (children)'
/pahit/ or /pait/	'bitter'

It resembles the sound in English hat, but occurs after vowels as well as before vowels.

This phoneme is represented in the writing system by the letter H, h.

/habis/	habis	'finished'
/sudah/	sudah	'already'
/mahal/	mahal	'expensive'
/lahir/	lahir	'bear (children)'
/pahit/	pahit	'bitter'

1.3 Nasal Consonants

1.3.1 /m/

There is a phoneme which is a bilabial voiced

oral stop with nasal release /m/. It occurs initially and finally in the syllable.

It resembles the sound in English _me_, but is completely voiced.

It is represented in the writing system by the letter _M_, _m_.

/malam/	malam	'night'
/minum/	minum	'drink'

1.3.2 /n/

There is a phoneme which is an apico-dental or apico-alveolar voiced oral stop with nasal release /n/. It occurs initially or finally in the syllable.

It resembles the sound in English _no_, but is completely voiced.

It is represented in the writing system by the letter _N_, _n_. The letter _N_, _n_ is also used in the digraphs _nj_ (1.3.3) and _ng_ (1.3.4).

/kanan/	kanan	'right'
/nanti/	nanti	'later'

1.3.3 /ñ/

There is a phoneme which is a lamino-dental or lamino-alveolar voiced palatalized oral stop with nasal release /ñ/. It occurs initially in the syllable.

It resembles the sound which occurs when the English words _can you_ are pronounced quickly.

It is represented in the writing system by the digraph _Nj_, _nj_ (Indonesian) or the digraph _Ny_, _ny_ (Malay).

/ñañi/	njanji (I) nyanyi (M)	'sing'
/ñoña/	njonja (I) nyonya (M)	'married woman'

1.3.4 /ŋ̧/

There is a phoneme which is a dorso-velar voiced oral stop with nasal release /ŋ̧/. It occurs initially and finally in the syllable.

It resembles the sound at the end of the English song.

It is represented in the writing system by the digraph Ng, ng; this digraph is never to be interpreted as representing the sequence of phonemes /n/ followed by /g/; this sequence does not occur within the same word. Nor is it to be interpreted as the phoneme /ŋ̧/ followed by the phoneme /g/; this sequence of phonemes is represented in the writing system by the sequence of letters ngg.

/ŋ̧aŋ̧a/	nganga	'agape'
/taŋ̧guŋ̧/	tanggung	'guaranteed'

1.4 The trill /r/

There is an apical post-dental trill phoneme /r/. It occurs initially and finally in the syllable.

It resembles the trilled or rolled sound in Scottish or Spanish.

It may consist of a single flap of the trill, or of a prolonged trill, but is usually two or three taps. It is fully voiced initially and medially in the utterance, but may be voiceless and somewhat fricative before pause.

This phoneme is represented in the writing system by the letter R, r.

/ratus/	ratus	'hundred'
/kabar/	kabar	'news'

1.5 The lateral /l/

There is an apical post-dental lateral phoneme /l/. It occurs initially and finally in the syllable.

It resembles the sound in English leap, never the sound in English peel, where the back of the tongue is raised.

It is represented in the writing system by the letter L, l.

/lalat/	lalat	'house-fly'
/mahal/	mahal	'expensive'

1.6 Semivowels

1.6.1 /y/

There is a semivowel phoneme /y/. This phoneme includes all glides from the position of the vowel /i/ to the position of a following vowel, and all glides from the position of a preceding vowel to the position of the vowel /i/. It consequently occurs initially and finally in the syllable.

/yakin/	'certain'
/yunani/	'Greek'
/hëlay/	'sheet (of paper)'

It somewhat resembles the sound in English year.

This phoneme is represented in the writing system by the letter J, j (Indonesian) or the letter Y, y (Malay) when it occurs before a vowel. It is represented by the letter I, i when it occurs after a vowel; actually it occurs only after a, or very rarely, o.

/yakin/	jakin (I) yakin (M)	'certain'
/yunani/	Junani (I) Yunani (M)	'Greek'
/suŋay/	sungai	'river'
/hëlay/	helai	'sheet (of paper)'

1.6.2 /w/

There is a semivowel phoneme /w/. This phoneme includes all glides from the position of the vowel /u/ to the position of a following vowel, and all glides from the position of a preceding vowel to the position of the vowel /u/. It consequently occurs initially and finally in the syllable.

It somewhat resembles the sound in English woo.

This phoneme is represented in the writing system by the letter W, w when it occurs before a vowel. It is represented by the letter U, u when it occurs after a vowel; actually it occurs only after a.

/warna/	warna	'color'
/bahwa/	bahwa	'that'
/kalaw/	kalau	'if'

1.7 Vowels, General

The distribution of the vowel phonemes and their allophones is an area in which there is a great deal of variation. It would be quite impossible to describe the vowel phonemes in a way which would be acceptable to all speakers.

Since this is a reference grammar, and will probably be used in connection with written materials, the vowel phonemes described here are those reflected by the writing system. This is a system of pronunciation which is to be found in Central Sumatra and in the Malay Peninsula. (Speakers of other local languages, especially the Javanese, are less likely to use a pronunciation of this type.)

There are six vowels / i, e, ë, a, u, o /.

In some areas, each of these six vowels has only the one pronunciation in all positions in the word. This is exceptional, however.

In the six-vowel system, each vowel except /ë/ usually has two chief allophones: one is higher (the mouth is slightly less open, and the tongue is consequently higher in relation to the roof of the mouth); the other is lower (the mouth is slightly more open and the tongue is relatively lower). The lower allophone occurs in closed syllables, that is, in syllables ending in a consonant. The higher allophone occurs in open syllables, that is, in syllables which end with that vowel. However, a vowel in an open syllable, and followed in the same word by the same vowel in a closed syllable, occurs in the lower allophone rather than the higher.

The six vowel phonemes with their allophones are given here, the higher allophone being marked by ' and the lower allophone by , as necessary.

	Front	Central	Back
High	/i/ : i' : i,		/u/ : u' : u,
Mid	/e/ : e' : e,	/ë/	/o/ : o' : o,
Low		/a/ : a' : a,	

This is the system which will be described here.

The various local languages have differing phonemic systems. Javanese, for example, has eight vowels: / i é ê ë a u ó ô /. These can be charted as follows:

	Front	Central	Back
High	i		u
Higher mid	é		ó
		ë	
Lower mid	ê		ô
Low		a	

It is easy to understand how a Javanese speaker, accustomed to distinguishing eight vowels in his own language, will tend to do so in Bahasa Indonesia also. The overriding tendency is to equate the Javanese /i/ with the higher allophone of the Indonesian /i/, that is, with ^{a}/i'/, to equate the Javanese /e/ both with the lower allophone of the Indonesian /i/ and with the higher allophone of the Indonesian /e/, that is, with both ^{a}/i,/ and ^{a}/e'/, and also to equate the Javanese /ê/ with the lower allophone of the Indonesian /e/, that is, with ^{a}/e,/. A similar pattern governs the equation of Javanese /u/ with Indonesian ^{a}/u'/, Javanese /ó/ with Indonesian ^{a}/u,/ and ^{a}/o'/, and Javanese /ô/ with Indonesian ^{a}/o,/.

In addition to phonemic interference from local languages, the possibility of phonemic interference from Dutch must also be considered. For many older speakers, Dutch was the medium of instruction in their education, and Dutch also makes phonemic distinctions which cut across the allophonic patterning of Indonesian.

Enough Indonesian speakers, with differing language backgrounds, distinguish eight vowels to make it necessary to give serious consideration to the question as to whether Bahasa Indonesia should not actually be described as having eight vowels. Clearcut contrasts between a higher and a lower o-sound continue to be difficult to find with many speakers, however. In addition, though many speakers distinguish three vowels similar to the Javanese /i, é, ȇ/, the distribution of a distinctive é in the vocabulary of the language fluctuates to such an extent (a survey was taken of some thirty speakers of Indonesian residing in the United States), that it would be impractical to try to reflect it in a reference grammar of this sort and at this point in history.

1.7.1 /i/

There is a high front unrounded vowel phoneme /i/.

/i/ has two chief allophones.

a) In a closed syllable it is a sound very much like the English vowel sound in bit. /sakit/

In an open syllable followed immediately by a closed syllable, especially if the following syllable contains the same vowel, it may also be a sound very much like the English vowel sound in bit. /titik/

b) In other open syllables, it is a sound very much like the English diphthong in bee, starting somewhat higher (that is, with the tongue closer to the roof of the mouth at the front) and with only a slight off-glide.

This phoneme is represented in the writing system by the letter I, i.

/sakit/	sakit	'sore'
/titik/	titik	'point'
/qisi/	isi	'contents'

/qibu/	ibu	'mother'

There are certain fluctuations in the spellings of words in which the letter i is involved.

Some words in which there is the phoneme /i/ in the second syllable of the root and in which this syllable is closed, also occur in an alternate form in which the phoneme /e/ occurs instead of /i/. The choice as to which form will be used is determined by the predilection of the individual speaker, but the form with /i/ is the more formal. There is, therefore, the possibility that some words will be spelled with either i or e; this alternation is more common in Malay than in Indonesian.

/qadik/ or /qadek/	adik or adek	'younger brother or sister'

(For alternations of the spelling ai with the spelling e, see 1.7.6).

1.7.2 /u/

There is a high back rounded vowel phoneme /u/.

/u/ has two chief allophones.

a) In a closed syllable it has a sound somewhat like the English vowel sound in book but somewhat higher (that is, with the high point of the tongue closer to the roof of the mouth at the back). /takut/

In an open syllable followed immediately by a closed syllable containing the same vowel, it may have this same sound. /tutup/

b) In other open syllables, it is a sound very much like the diphthong in the English boo, starting somewhat higher (that is, with the high point of the tongue closer to the roof of the mouth at the back) and with only a slight off-glide. /satu/

This phoneme is now customarily represented in the writing system by the letter U, u in both Indonesian and Malay. During the Dutch regime in Indonesia the customary representation was the digraph Oe, oe; this spelling is retained by some writers, but is most evident now in proper names. e.g. Soenjono.

/takut/	takut (takoet)	'afraid'
/tutup/	tutup (toetoep)	'close'
/satu/	satu (satoe)	'one'

There are certain fluctuations in the spellings of words in which the letter u is involved. Some words in which there is the phoneme /u/ in the second syllable of the root, and in which this syllable is closed, also occur in an alternate form in which the phoneme /o/ occurs instead of the phoneme /u/. The choice as to which form will be used is largely determined by the predilection of the individual speakers, but the form with /u/ is felt to be the more formal. There is, therefore, the possibility that some words will be spelled with either /u/ or /o/; the variant with /o/ is more common in Malay.

/këbun/ or	kebun or	'garden, orchard'
/këbon/	kebon	

(For alternations of the spelling au with o, see 1.7.6).

1.7.3 /e/

There is a mid front unrounded vowel phoneme /e/.

/e/ has two chief allophones.

a) In a closed syllable it is a sound very

much like the English vowel sound in *bet*, /pendeq/. In an open syllable followed immediately by a closed syllable, especially one containing the same vowel phoneme, it is also a sound very much like the English vowel sound in *bet*, /bebeq/.

b) In other open syllables, it is a sound very much like the English diphthong in *bay*, starting somewhat higher (that is, with the tongue closer to the roof of the mouth in front) and with only a slight off-glide. /sate/ /sore/

This phoneme is represented in the writing system by the letter *E*, *e*. Formerly, it was written *É*, é in Indonesian in order to distinguish it from /ë/ which was written *E*, *e*; now no attempt at distinction is made. It is customarily written *E*, *e* in Malay, and /ë/ is distinguished from it by being written *Ĕ*, *ĕ*. For fluctuations in spelling involving the letter *E*, *e*, see 1.7.1, 1.7.4 and 1.7.6.

/pendeq/	pendek (péndék)	'short'
/bebeq/	bebek (bébék)	'duck'
/sate/	sate (saté)	'shishkebob'
/sore/	sore (soré)	'evening'

1.7.4 /ë/

There is a mid-central unrounded vowel phoneme /ë/.

With certain speakers, the occurrence of /ë/ may be predictable, because no clusters of consonants occur within the syllable in their language, and this vowel is introduced to break up such consonant clusters as are found in the speech of other speakers. Thus, such borrowed words as *klas*, 'class', *glas*, 'glass', *stop*, 'stop', and *listrik*, 'electricity' are likely to be pronounced as /këlas, gëlas, sëtop, listërik/. With other speakers, especially where there is the influence of a local language or the knowledge of a foreign language or both, this vowel is certainly not predictable. The individual is more likely to speak in such a way that this vowel must be regarded as a phoneme. Thus there may be considerable variation between speakers, or between different utterances of the same speaker, in the occurrences of this vowel in particular words.

/këlas/ or /klas/	'class'
/qënam/ or /qnam/	'four'

This vowel has a limited distribution in that it does not occur in the last syllable of a word in Indonesian (except in borrowings from Javanese and other local languages) and in that it is usually never stressed; some speakers stress it in closed penultimate syllables, however.

This phoneme /ë/ is represented in the writing system by the letter E, e in Indonesian, as is also the phoneme /e/; see 1.7.3. It is represented in Malay by Ĕ, ĕ.

The fluctuation in occurrence is also reflected in the orthography so that the spellings kelas and klas, gelas and glas, setop and stop, listrik and listerik are all to be found. The longer forms are usually preferred over the shorter.

For other fluctuations in orthography involving this vowel, see 1.7.6.

1.7.5 /o/

There is a mid back rounded vowel phoneme /o/.

/o/ has two chief allophones.

a) In a closed syllable it is a sound very much like the vowel in British English pot; that is, much closer to u than in the American English pot. /potlot/

In an open syllable followed immediately by a closed syllable containing the same vowel phoneme, it is also a sound of the same quality. /bodoh/

b) In other open syllables, it is a sound very much like the English diphthong in go, starting somewhat higher (that is, with the high point of the tongue closer to the roof of the mouth at the back) and with only a slight off-glide. /qoto/

This phoneme is represented in the writing system by the letter O, o. For fluctuations in spelling involving the letter O, o, see 1.7.2 and 1.7.6.

/qekor/	ekor	'tail'
/bodoh/	bodoh	'stupid'
/qoto/	oto	'auto'

1.7.6 /a/

There is a low central unrounded vowel phoneme /a/.

/a/ has two chief allophones.

a) In a closed syllable, it is a sound very much like the English vowel sound in baa but higher (that is, a little closer to the vowel sound in but). /dĕkat/

In an open syllable followed immediately by a closed syllable containing the same vowel phoneme, it is also this type of sound. /papan/

b) In other open syllables, it is a sound very much like the English sound in baa or bah, with the high point of tongue low in the mouth and midway between front and back; there may be a slight off-glide to a higher and more central position (that is, towards, but not attaining, the position of /ĕ/). /lama/

This phoneme is represented in the writing system by the letter A, a.

/dëkat/	dekat	'near'
/papan/	papan	'plank'
/lama/	lama	'ancient'

There are certain fluctuations in the spellings of words in which this letter is involved.

When the sequences /ay/ and /aw/ (spelled ai and au respectively) occur in one syllable of a word, the word usually has a variant form in which /ay/ is replaced by /e/ (spelled e) and /aw/ is replaced by /o/ (spelled o).

/suŋay/	sungai	or	/suŋe/	sunge	'river'
/panday/	pandai	or	/pande/	pande	'clever'
/hijaw/	hidjau	or	/hijo/	hidjo	'green'
/pulaw/	pulau	or	/pulo/	pulo	'island'

The forms with /ay/ and /aw/ are the more formal, and therefore the spellings sungai, pandai and hidjau, pulau are preferred.

Some local dialects have words which have a vowel similar to /ë/ in the last syllable where /ë/ does not customarily occur in Indonesian; in the corresponding words in formal Indonesian, the vowel /a/ occurs. Some speakers, however, continue to use the local vowel /ë/, and may also write such words with the letter e.

/sumbër/ or /sumbar/	sumber or sumbar	'well'
/garëm/ or /garam/	garem or garam	'salt'

The spelling with A, a is to be preferred on the formal level.

1.8 The Syllable

Syllables may be open (terminated by a vowel) or closed (terminated by a consonant).

An open syllable (CV) customarily consists of any one consonant phoneme (C) followed by any one vowel phoneme (V).

A closed syllable (CVĆ) has the same structure as the open syllable, except that the vowel is followed by any one of the following consonants: /p, t, k, q, f, s, h, r, l, y, w, m, n, ŋ/.

Speakers who are familiar with foreign languages may, especially in using words borrowed from those languages, have syllables which begin with a cluster of consonants, but for other speakers it is more usual to reduce these clusters by inserting the vowel /ë/ so as to produce the syllable pattern described here.

listrik	listerik	'electricity'
strika	setrika or seterika	'flat iron'

The tendency to accept and pronounce initial consonant clusters is growing rapidly, however; the word <u>struktur</u> is almost never pronounced as more than two syllables.

1.9 Stress

The stress in Indonesian falls upon the second to last syllable of the word. If the second to last syllable contains the vowel /ë/, the stress will fall on the last syllable. The stress regularly falls on the last syllable of personal names when used vocatively, that is, for summoning the person.

This statement must be hedged about with many exceptions. In some of the local languages (e.g.

Atjinese) the stress regularly falls on the last syllable, and speakers of such languages may stress the last syllable in talking Indonesian. Some speakers shift the accent to the last syllable if the second to last contains the vowel /ë/ and is open (beli), but retain the stress on the second to last syllable if it is closed (kertas). The pattern of accenting the last syllable of the vocative seems to be general; it is this accentuation which induces the short forms of names in which only the last syllable is retained: Man for Suratman, La for Mala, etc. Other calls retain the last two syllables (Doman! - the newsvendor's cry for the paper Pedoman, etc.). A few names however, retain the penultimate syllable, if closed, or the penultimate syllable plus the initial consonant of the final syllable, perhaps because the final syllable is the same as that of many other names: Tin for Kartini.

The practice of stressing the second to last syllable of the root, and of maintaining this stress when suffixes are added, is regarded as foreign.

Enclitic forms (-lah, -pun, -kah) are not a part of the word and so do not condition a shift of the stress (másuk, másuklah; masúk! masúklah!)

The stressed syllables in Indonesian are only slightly louder than the unstressed syllables. All syllables are pronounced as fully when unstressed as when stressed, and there is no alteration of vowels in unstressed syllables. Syllables may be dropped entirely, but they are not slurred.

1.10 The Mora

The unit of rhythm (mora) in Indonesian is the syllable. All syllables are given the same amount of time in speaking so that the vowels in open syllables tend to be slightly longer than the vowels in closed syllables.

1.11 The Intonation

The intonation patterns of Indonesian cannot be discussed briefly; an extensive description of intonation is beyond the scope of this book.

M O R P H O L O G Y

2.0 Morphemes

The smallest components of a language which have a value within the language structure are the morphemes. The description of the morphemes and the manner in which they combine is the morphology.

There are two primary types of morphemes in Indonesian, roots (2.0.1) and affixes (2.0.2).

Roots are morphemes which occur independently, or which occur freely in combinations, whether in initial, medial or final position in an utterance.

Affixes are morphemes which are never independent, and which occur in a fixed relationship to a base. (A base is distinct from a root in the following way. A root always consists of a single root morpheme; a base consists of one or more morphemes, whether a single root, a reduplicated root, or a combination of roots in some morphological or syntactic arrangement, and either with or without affixes. A root is thus one possible form of base.) Affixes can be subclassified as prefixes, infixes and suffixes.

It will prove most convenient to describe the forms of the roots and affixes first, and to describe their structural function, either singly or in combination, later. The form of the root is discussed in Section 2.0.1, the form of the prefixes in 2.0.2, the form of the infixes in 2.0.3, and the form of the suffixes in 2.0.4. The organization of the discussion of the structural function is outlined in 2.0.5.

2.0.1 Roots

The Indonesian root typically consists of two syllables.

The first syllable consists of

a) a consonant plus a vowel, or

b) a consonant plus a vowel plus a nasal consonant having the same point of articulation as the initial consonant of the second syllable, or

c) a consonant plus a vowel plus the consonant r.

The second syllable consists of

a) a consonant plus a vowel, or

b) a consonant plus a vowel plus any of the consonants which occur in final position.

la-ri	ti-dur
bu-ka	ta-ngan
djam-bu	pim-pin
min-ta	ken-tang
tung-gu	tang-gal
ker-dja	per-nah

There are many roots, however, which do not follow the usual pattern. Such roots are frequently, but not necessarily, borrowings from other languages. The most notable other patterns are these.

2.0.1.1 Some roots have only one syllable. Examples are

es	(Dutch)	'ice'
mas		'gold'
pak	(Dutch)	'pack'
sah	(Arabic)	'valid, legal'
tik	(Dutch)	'type(write)'
tjap	(Persian)	'stamp, seal'
tjat	(Chinese)	'paint'

2.0.1.2 Other roots have three or more syllables. Examples are

bendera	(Portuguese)	'flag'
djendela	(Portuguese)	'window'
ekonomi	(Dutch)	'economy'
listerik	(Dutch)	'electricity'
manusia	(Sanskrit)	'human being'
organisasi	(Dutch)	'organization'
pustaka	(Sanskrit)	'book, literature'
republik	(Dutch)	'republic'
saudagar	(Persian)	'merchant'
tentera	(Sanskrit)	'army'

2.0.1.3 Occasionally a root has two syllables, but does not follow the specific patterns mentioned above. Examples are

bulbul	(Persian)	'nightingale'
ikrar	(Arabic)	'promise'
mesdjid	(Arabic)	'mosque'
potlot	(Dutch)	'pencil'
Sabtu	(Arabic)	'Saturday'
tanpa	(Javanese)	'without'

2.0.1.4 It also happens, of course, that roots which conform to the basic Indonesian pattern are nonetheless borrowings. Such roots may have conformed to the basic pattern in any case. Others have been modified so that they now conform to this pattern.

anggur	(Persian)	'wine'
guru	(Sanskrit)	'teacher'
hakim	(Arabic)	'judge'
kamar	(Dutch)	'room'
kapal	(Tamil)	'ship'
pasar	(Persian)	'market'
peti	(Tamil)	'box'
sebab	(Arabic)	'reason'
sehat	(Arabic)	'healthy'
Senin	(Arabic)	'Monday'

2.0.2 Prefixes

Prefixes occur before roots. Consequently they can occur only initially or medially in an utterance. There are a number of important and productive prefixes in Indonesian.

These prefixes are

ber-, *per-*, *ter-*
meN-, *peN-*
se-, *ke-*, *di-*

The prefixes which are here listed on any one line show the same patterns of variation in form, and so the forms of these prefixes can be described together.

2.0.2.1 The prefixes *ber-*, *per-*, *ter-*

The prefixes *ber-*, *per-*, and *ter-* are cited here in their commonly occurring form.

batas	berbatas perbatasan terbatas
angkat	berangkat perangkatan terangkat

kenan	berkenan perkenan terkenan

Before bases beginning with _r_, they have the forms _be_-, _pe_- and _te_-.

renang	berenang perenang terenang-renang
rasa	berasa perasa terasa
ribut	beribut peribut teribut

Before bases whose first syllable ends in -_er_, these prefixes also have the forms _be_-, _pe_- and _te_-.

kerdja	bekerdja pekerdja tekerdjakan
perkara	beperkara
serta	beserta peserta
ternak	beternak and berternak peternak

In other cases also, especially in colloquial style, a variant _be_-, _pe_-, _te_- may occur where, according to the above description, the variant _ber_-, _per_-, _ter_- is to be expected. The occurrence of _be_- with a particular base does not necessarily indicate that _pe_- will occur instead of _per_-, or _te_- instead of _ter_- and vice versa. No pattern for this phenomenon has been observed.

gadai	pegadaian
gunung	bergunung pegunungan
djuang	berdjuang pedjuang perdjuangan

Before a certain few roots, the prefixes have the forms bel-, pel-, and tel-.

adjar	beladjar peladjar
undjur	belundjur

(It has sometimes been stated that this form of the prefix occurs before roots which begin with a vowel in the orthography, and which have an r at some later point in the root. Actually, there are many more roots of this description before which the prefixes have the forms ber-, per- and ter- than those before which they have the forms bel-, pel-, and tel-.)

2.0.2.2 The prefixes meN- and peN-

The prefixes meN-, peN are cited here in a form which is intended to show that all variants of each of these morphemes begin with me- or pe- respectively, and that certain nasal sounds may follow, depending on the base to which the prefixes are added.

Before bases beginning with b, f or v, the variants mem- and pem- occur.

buka	membuka pembuka
buat	membuat pembuat

batja	membatja pembatja
fitnah	memfitnah
veto	memveto

Before bases beginning with *p*, the variants are also *mem*- and *pem*-, but a variant form of the base occurs in which the initial *p* is not present.

pindjam	memindjam pemindjam
pakai	memakai pemakai

With certain bases, clearly borrowed from other languages, the *p* may, however, be retained.

potret	memotret or mempotret pemotret or pempotret
protes	memrotes or memprotes
proklamasi	memproklamasi
propaganda	mempropaganda

In the case of bases beginning with the prefix *per*-, the *p* of the prefix is retained.

besar	memperbesar
tuan	mempertuan

Before bases beginning with *d*, *tj*, *dj*, *sj* and *z*, the variants *men*- and *pen*- occur.

dapat	mendapat pendapat

tjari	mentjari pentjari
djual	mendjual pendjual
ziarah	menziarahi
sjak	mensjak

Before some bases beginning with _sj_, the variants _menj-_ and _penj-_ occur, and a variant form of the root occurs in which the initial _sj_ is not present.

sjair	menjairkan penjairan

Similarly, before some bases beginning with _tj_, the variants _menj-_ and _penj-_ may occur, and a variant form of the root occurs in which the initial _tj_ is not present.

tjukur	mentjukur or menjukur pentjukur or penjukur
tjutji	mentjutji or menjutji

Before bases beginning with _t_, the variants are also _men-_ and _pen-_, but a variant form of the base occurs in which the initial _t_ is not present.

tulis	menulis penulis
tolong	menolong penolong

With certain bases, clearly borrowed from other languages, the _t_ may, however, be retained.

terdjemah	menterdjemahkan penterdjemah

tafsir	menafsirkan or mentafsirkan penafsiran or pentafsiran

Before bases beginning with s, the variant menj- and penj- occur, and a variant form of the root occurs in which the initial s is not present.

sapu	menjapu penjapu
susun	menjusun penjusun
sakit	menjakitkan penjakit

With certain bases, clearly borrowed from other languages, the s may, however, be retained, and the prefix has the form men-.

seleksi	menseleksi or menjeleksi
sita	mensita or menjita

Before bases beginning with g, ch, h, or, in the orthography, any vowel, the variants meng- and peng- occur.

gosok	menggosok penggosok
chianat	mengchianati pengchianat
hitung	menghitung penghitung
adjar	mengadjar pengadjar
isi	mengisi pengisi

Before bases beginning with k, the variants are also meng- and peng-, but a variant form of the root occurs in which the initial k is not present.

kirim	mengirim pengirim
kajuh	mengajuh pengajuh
kantuk	mengantuk pengantuk

With certain bases, clearly borrowed from other languages, the k may, however, be retained.

klise	mengklisekan
komentar	mengomentari or mengkomentari

In all other cases, the variants are me- and pe-, with occasional exceptions.

latih	melatih pelatih
rokok	merokok perokok
naik	menaik penaik
njanji	menjanji penjanji
nganga	menganga penganga
minta	meminta peminta
warna	mewarnakan

Monosyllabic bases are, in general, susceptible of two treatments. Either the one syllable is retained in its entirety, and the appropriate variant of meN- and peN- prefixed to it, or it is made disyllabic by the prefixing of the vowel e-, and this disyllabic base is then prefixed with meng- or peng- in accordance with the description given above for roots beginning with a vowel in the orthography.

tjap	mentjapkan	mengetjapkan pengetjapan
pak	mempak	mengepak pengepak
tik	mentik	mengetik
sah	mensahkan	mengesahkan pengesahan

When the prefix meN- is added to a reduplicated root (full reduplication only), the first item of the reduplication receives the full prefix in the form appropriate to its initial phoneme. The second item can be said to have the same form except that the first syllable is dropped. This is tantamount to saying, for most cases, that the prefix does not appear at all, since the prefix itself forms the first syllable. But, in cases where the verb root begins with /p, t, s, k/ and occasionally /c̃, s/, and these consonants are not present in the prefixed form, the nasal consonant of the prefix becomes the initial consonant of the second syllable, and so is retained. In the case of verb roots which begin, in the orthography, with a vowel, but, in certain pronunciations, with the phoneme /q/ and in others with a vowel, the nasal consonant is retained by some speakers and omitted by others, but the omission is more common.

masak	memasak-masak

balik	membalik-balik
djadi	mendjadi-djadi
gosok	menggosok-gosok
tjari	mentjari-tjari
kira	mengira-ngira or mengira-ira
pikir	memikir-mikir
tari	menari-nari
indjak	mengindjak-indjak

2.0.2.3 The prefixes se-, ke- and di-

The prefixes se-, ke- and di- have only the one form.

(In a very few words, there is what appears to be the prefix se- or the prefix ke- followed by a root beginning with a stop consonant, while between the prefix and the stop consonant is a nasal having the same point of articulation as the following stop. This is, in some cases, a relic of a morphological process which seems to have been relatively common in the languages of the Austronesian family many centuries ago, or, in other cases, it represents a fairly common Sanskrit prefix in words borrowed from that language. This formation is not productive in contemporory Indonesian.

diri	sendiri kendiri
barang	sembarang
karut	sengkarut
purna	sempurna)

2.0.3 Infixes

The infix is not a common morphological device in contemporary Indonesian. It is possible to recognize three: -el-, -em- and -er-.

The infix occurs after the first consonant of the root, (there are no initial consonant clusters in the forms in which infixes occur) and is followed by the first vowel of the root. Occasionally forms are found which appear to have more than one infix. In such cases the second infix follows immediately after the first. Such forms are not widely accepted, and, when they are, the speaker of Indonesian rarely conceives of them as containing two infixes. Indeed, the speaker of Indonesian rarely conceives of a form as containing even one infix, but simply accepts the infixed form as a type of root-form.

getar	gemetar
guruh	gemuruh
gigi	gerigi
gosok	gerosok
tapak	telapak
gembung	gelembung
(getuk)	gemeretuk

2.0.4 Suffixes

The suffixes exhibit little variation in form. There are three widely-used Indonesian suffixes. These are

a) -an

b) -kan

c) -i

One other Indonesian suffix, rather restricted in use, is

d) -anda/-nda

The remaining suffixes occur in borrowings from Arabic or Sanskrit, but, because there has been such heavy borrowing from these languages, these suffixes are identifiable as suffixes in Indonesian also. They are

e) -at

f) -i/-wi

g) -a and -i

h) -man/-wan and -wati

The suffixes -an, -kan and -i are living suffixes in contemporary Indonesian; they have a wide distribution, and are still used to form new words.

2.0.4.1 The suffix -kan has one form.

memindjam	memindjamkan
mengadjar	mengadjarkan
mengisi	mengisikan
menaik	menaikkan

2.0.4.2 The suffix -i has one form.

air	mengairi
atas	mengatasi
kenal	mengenali

While the orthographic form is -i, the phonemic form is /-qi/. Thus, this suffix is always pronounced as a full vowel distinct from any vowel which may precede it, even though, in the orthography, it may seem to form a diphthong with the preceding vowel. The glottal stop /q/ is only weakly articulated in this position, since the suffix is rarely added to roots ending in /i/, and so the vowels are generally dissimilar.

nama	menamai	/mĕnamaqi/
lalu	melalui	/mĕlaluqi/
punja	mempunjai	/mĕmpuñaqi/

If the suffix is added to a base ending with k in the orthography (/q/ in the pronunciation), then the combination of glottal stops may be resolved into /q/ by some speakers, and by others into /k/.

duduk	menduduki	/mĕnduduqi, mĕnduduki/
rabuk	merabuki	/mĕrabuqi, mĕrabuki/

2.0.4.3 The suffix -an has one form.

tulis	tulisan
pasang	pasangan
minum	minuman

While the orthographic form is -an, the phonemic form is /-qan/. Thus, this suffix is always pronounced as a distinct syllable. The glottal stop /q/ is most clearly articulated between similar vowels, and less clearly between dissimilar vowels.

ribu	ribuan	/ribuqan/
ada	keadaan	/kĕadaqan/

When this suffix is added to bases ending with k in the orthography (/q/ in the pronunciation), the orthography is not affected, but the pronunciation is /q/, or, for some speakers, /k/.

duduk	pendudukan	/pĕnduduqan/
		/pĕndudukan/

masuk	kemasukan	/këmasuqan/ /këmasukan/

2.0.4.4 The suffix -anda has two forms: -anda and -nda. The former is usually added to roots ending in a consonant, the latter to roots ending in a vowel. There are, however, a number of forms which show other combinations.

anak	anakanda, ananda
ajah	ajahanda, ajahnda, ajanda
paman	pamanda
adik	adinda
kakak	kakanda
nenek	nenenda
ibu	ibunda

The suffix -i/-wi has the alternate form -i, which occurs after roots ending in a consonant, and the alternate form -wi, which occurs after roots ending with a vowel.

firdaus	firdausi
dunia	duniawi

The suffix -man/-wan also has alternate forms. The form -wan occurs after roots ending in the vowel a; the form -man occurs elsewhere.

harta	hartawan
budi	budiman

The remaining suffixes have one form only.

2.0.5 Morphological Combinations

The following description of the combinations of roots and affixes is intended to be exhaustive of those cases where the combination has an independent value. Morphologically complex forms exist which show other combinations, but these are combinations of the combinations listed here; that is, a form which is already morphologically complex may be used as the base for constructing still another form by the addition of more prefixes and suffixes. The effect of the whole is the sum of the effects of the two independent combinations taken in order. Thus, from the root angkat, the intransitive verb berangkat 'depart' is formed. This morphologically complex unit is in turn combined with the prefix meN- and the suffix -kan to make a causative verb memberangkatkan 'to cause to depart, send away, dismiss.' This last form, then, is not the result of one unitary morphological process, but the result of two consecutive morphological processes. In the discussion that follows, forms resulting from consecutive application of morphological processes will be included under the discussion of the latest of these processes to be applied.

The following order has been selected for this description.

Combinations involving roots alone. (2.1)

Combinations involving roots and suffixes but no prefixes. (2.2)

Combinations with or without suffixes involving:

the prefix ber- (2.3)

the prefix meN- (2.4)

the prefix ter- (2.5)

the prefix per- (2.6)

the prefix peN- (2.7)

the prefix ke- (2.8)

the prefix se- (2.9)

2.1 Morphological Combinations of Roots

Indonesian roots combine morphologically in two chief ways. These are reduplication (2.1.1) and compounding (2.1.2). Infixing will also be discussed at this point (2.1.3) since the use of infixing in contemporary Indonesian is rather a process of root-formation than of derivation or inflection.

2.1.1 Reduplication

Reduplication is of three types; there is full reduplication (2.1.1.1), partial reduplication (2.1.1.2), and imitative reduplication, or imitation (2.1.1.3). Forms reduplicated in one manner are not again reduplicated in that manner or in either of the other manners.

2.1.1.1 Full Reduplication

In full reduplication the entire root is repeated without modification.

orang	'human being'
orang-orang	'human beings'
djalan	'walk, go'
djalan-djalan	'walk about, go here and there'

In the Indonesian orthography, full reduplication is frequently indicated by placing the number 2 after the form to be reduplicated, either on the line or raised above the line. In most cases only the root is to be reduplicated, but in other cases some or all of the affixes may be included in the reduplication. There is no fixed convention for indicating these differences. Thus, <u>orang-orang</u> will appear as <u>orang2</u>, and <u>djalan-djalan</u> as <u>djalan2</u>.

2.1.1.2 Partial Reduplication

In partial reduplication the first consonant of the root, followed by the vowel /ĕ/, is prefixed to the root.

laki	'male'
lelaki	'male, man, husband'
tapi	'but'
tetapi	'but'

This type of reduplication is functionally the same as full reduplication, though less common in occurrence, and seems to be readily convertible into full reduplication on all occasions; full reduplication is not, however, readily convertible into partial reduplication, and many speakers avoid partial reduplication for the most part.

2.1.1.3 Imitative Reduplication

In imitative reduplication there is, either before or after the main root, a repetition of a rootlike form, which generally does not exist independently. The quasi-root resembles the root in part, but, while certain patterns of differences are observable, there does not seem to be any means of predicting which pattern of difference will be used in any particular case, and there does not seem to be any specific meaning which can be ascribed to any particular pattern of difference.

The commonest patterns of difference are the following:

a) The consonants remain the same, but the vowels change to some extent.

In a few cases, one vowel changes.

belat	'screen'
belat-belit	'underhanded'
desus	'rumor'
desas-desus	'rumors, whispering'

More frequently, both vowels change, and they usually follow the regular pattern /o/-/a/-/a/-/i/ or /u/-/a/-/a/-/i/.

balik	'reverse'
bolak-balik	'to and fro'
djongkat-djangkit	'bob up and down'
ganti	'substitute'
gonta-ganti	'reciprocal'
kutjar-katjir	'in disorder'
kupat-kapit	'dangling limply'
umbang	'float'
umbang-ambing	'drift to and fro'

b) The vowels tend to remain the same, but the consonants change in part.

tjerai	'part, sever'
tjerai-berai	'disperse'
tjoreng	'scratch'
tjoreng-moreng	'full of scratches'
sajur	'vegetable'
sajur-majur	'various sorts of vegetables'

c) Both consonants and vowels change in part, so that the degree of similarity may be considerably reduced.

erot	'crooked'
erang-erot	'zig-zag'
petjah	'smashed'
petjah-belah	'pottery; shattered'
porak-parik	'disorder; in disorder'
porak-peranda	'in disorder'
sabur	'vague, dim'
sabur-limbur	'confused, dusky'

Some examples of imitative reduplication are common and are used in formal Indonesian. Others are less common. By no means all of the forms listed in the more comprehensive dictionaries are familiar to all speakers of Indonesian, or, if familiar, they are not likely to be used in any but colloquial speech.

Of the three types of reduplication, only full reduplication is of importance in the formal language.

2.1.1.4 Reduplicated bases occur in almost all circumstances in which unreduplicated bases occur. They occur both with and without affixes (2.1.1.9).

In the majority of cases the meaning of the reduplicated form is the same as that of the unreduplicated form but with an added connotation of variety, randomness, or repetition.

2.1.1.5 Reduplication of Nouns

a) The reduplication of any countable noun produces a form which is specifically plural. The unreduplicated form is not specific; it may be singular or plural. There is some question as to whether the reduplicated form denotes simple plurality or whether it denotes both plurality and variety. Undoubtedly, speakers from different areas observe different usages.

buku	'book, or books'
buku-buku	'books, or different kinds of books'
medja	'table, or tables'
medja-medja	'tables, or different kinds of tables'

b) In some cases the reduplication of a noun produces another noun which has a related meaning. Thus, <u>mata</u> 'eye' co-occurs with <u>mata-mata</u> 'spy' that is, a person who is as another eye. Similar examples are

anak	'child'
anak-anak	'baby'
bantal	'pillow'
bantal-bantal	'railway tie'
bahan	'raw materials'
bahan-bahan	'ingredient'
djala	'fishing net'
djala-djala	'small net such as a hairnet'

c) Sometimes there is a reduplicated noun which has no observable connection in meaning with the unreduplicated noun.

ambai	'scoop net for fishing'
ambai-ambai	'a kind of ocean crab'

d) Nouns which refer to points of time, when reduplicated, produce adverbial expressions.

pagi	'morning'
pagi-pagi	'early in the morning'

malam	'darkness'
malam-malam	'at night'
fadjar	'dawn'
fadjar-fadjar	'at dawn'
siang	'daylight'
siang-siang	'at noon, early afternoon'

2.1.1.6 Reduplication of Adjectives

Reduplication also occurs to some extent in adjectives.

In Malay, the reduplication of an adjective serves to intensify its meaning.

besar	'big'
besar-besar	'extremely big'

but this device is not common in Indonesian.

A reduplicated adjective modifying a noun can be used to indicate that the noun is plural.

rumah besar	'big house'
rumah besar-besar	'big houses'

This device would seem to be a matter of particular style rather than of general structure, and is not commonly met with outside of certain writers.

2.1.1.7 Reduplication of Verb Roots

The reduplication of a verb root usually adds a connotation of variety, multiplicity or randomness. In particular, imitative reduplication emphasizes the connotation of randomness and lack of specific purpose.

djalan	'walk'
djalan-djalan	'stroll'

memasak	'cook'
memasak-masak	'do the cooking'
djongkat-djangkit	'wobble, bob up and down'

2.1.1.8 Reduplication as a Means of Deriving Adverbials

The reduplication of a root which is associated with one form-class may produce a form which belongs to another form-class, particularly the class of adverbs. Examples of the reduplication of nouns referring to time periods have been given above. The following are examples of reduplicated verb bases.

diam	'be silent'
diam-diam	'secretly, on the sly'
tiba	'arrive'
tiba-tiba	'suddenly'
kira	'guess'
kira-kira	'at a guess'
masak	'ripe, mature, cooked'
masak-masak	'thoroughly, maturely'
tjoba	'try'
tjoba-tjoba	'tentatively'

2.1.1.9 Reduplication with Affixes

Reduplicated forms accept affixes in much the same way as unreduplicated forms. The affix may occur with both parts of the reduplicated form, or only with one. Prefixes may occur with the first or second part or both. Infixes occur, though rarely, in the second part. Suffixes ordinarily occur only with the second part.

bagai	'kind, sort'
berbagai-bagai	'of all kinds'
ganti	'substitute'
ganti-berganti	'alternate with each other'
berganti-ganti	'alternate with each other'
kenal	'know'
berkenal-kenalan	'be acquainted with each other'
kenal-mengenal	'get to know each other'
masak	'cook'
memasak-masak	'do the cooking'
masak-memasak	'cookery'
bagus	'beautiful'
mebagus-baguskan	'flatter'
tari	'dance'
menari-nari	'hop, skip and jump'
takut	'afraid'
menakut-nakuti	'intimidate'
mempertakut-takuti	'intimidate'
minta	'ask'
peminta-minta	'beggar'
henti	'stop'
terhenti-henti	'halting, intermittent'
kali	'time'
sekali-kali	'from time to time'
sekali-sekali	'once in a while'
hari	'day'
sehari-harian	'the whole day through'

merah	'red'
kemerah-merahan	'reddish'
harga	'price'
harga-menghargai	'have respect for each other'

2.1.2 Compounding

Compounding is of two chief types: simple juxtaposition (2.1.2.1) and morphological binding (2.1.2.2).

2.1.2.1 Simple Juxtaposition

Simple juxtaposition is the arrangement of roots in series. Such a juxtaposition does not produce a simple syntactic collocation, however. If the combination were simply a syntactic collocation, its meaning would be predictable as the sum of the meanings of the components plus the meaning of the syntactic arrangement in which they can be construed as occurring. The compound, however, has a meaning which is other than a simple combination of the elements represented. In addition, the compound is inseparable and cannot be interrupted by morphological or syntactic elements. Nor can other forms be freely substituted for any members of a compound without reducing it to a syntactic collocation.

ibu	'mother'
bapak	'father'
ibu bapak	'parents'
tanah	'earth'
air	'water'
tanah air	'native land'
pandjang	'long'
tangan	'arm, hand'
pandjang tangan	'light-fingered'

naik	'ascend, mount'
hadji	'pilgrim to Mecca, pilgrimage to Mecca'
naik hadji	'go on a pilgrimage to Mecca'

The collocation of two nouns, as in ibu bapak, has the syntactic value of making the second noun modify the first. The syntactic collocation ibu bapak therefore means 'the mother of the father'. The juxtaposition of ibu bapak in a compound, however, produces a unit which means 'parents'.

The collocation of an adjective and a noun, as in pandjang tangan, has no specific syntactic value. As a syntactic collocation it has no meaning; (if the order were reversed, the adjective would modify the noun and that collocation would mean 'long arm'); as a compound, however, pandjang tangan means 'light-fingered, given to petty thievery'.

There is no formal means of distinguishing between compounds and collocations except that compounds are syntactically inseparable, whereas the items in a syntactic collocation are more loosely associated. That is the only difference. The orthography generally writes the members of the compound separately as if they had no more than a syntactic connection with each other; occasionally a hyphen may occur, but this is unusual. Orally, the patterns of stress and intonation show no consistent difference between collocations and compounds.

2.1.2.2 Morphologically Bound Compounds

Morphologically bound compounds are formed when an affix, ordinarily added to a simple root or to a base consisting of a root with other affixes, is added to a syntactic collocation, thus binding the whole into an inseparable compound.

ber-	'characterized by'
tanam	'plant'

padi	'rice'
bertanam padi	'characterized by the planting of rice, making a living as a rice farmer'
ke- -an	(noun formant)
tidak	'not'
adil	'just'
ketidakadilan	'injustice'
di- -kan	(causative verb formant, passive)
ke	'to, towards'
Djepang	'Japan'
dike Djepangkan	'sent to Japan'

Again, the orthography does not mark these compounds in any fixed manner. The affixes are regularly written together with the immediately contiguous form, but the other members of the compound are more usually written with spaces between them.

The various morphologically bound compounds are discussed under the morphological combination which binds them, so that <u>bertanam padi</u> is discussed under <u>ber</u>-, <u>ketidakadilan</u> under <u>ke</u>- -<u>an</u>, and so forth.

2.1.3 Infixes

Infixes are not a common morphological device in contemporary Indonesian. Since they are interior in the root, and since for many speakers they are now an established part of the root, they are discussed under root formations rather than in a separate section of their own.

It is now very difficult to assign particular values to the infixes. Not all speakers of Indonesian recognize all the infixed forms which may be found listed in dictionaries. And, of the forms which are listed, the definitions are not so consistently given that they show a clear pattern of meaning. Certainly the infixes do not have an inflectional value, as they have in Tagalog. And certainly the infixes are not used productively as they are in Javanese.

On the whole, it is perhaps easiest to accept the infixed forms as simply special kinds of unanalyzable roots. The words which are given here as containing infixes are representative of those few forms which most speakers of Indonesian accept fairly readily.

getar	'tremble'
gemetar	'tremble'
guruh	'thunder'
gemuruh	'like thunder'
gigi	'tooth'
gerigi	'toothed'
gosok	'rub'
gerosok	'shuffling'
gembung	'swollen'
gelembung	'swollen'
tapak	'palm of hand, sole of foot'
telapak	'palm of hand, sole of foot'
tundjuk	'index finger'
telundjuk	'index finger'
gerintjing	'jingle'
gemerintjing	'clanging'

The infix -em- in particular occurs in the second member of some reduplicated forms. Examples are:

turun	'descend'
turun-temurun	'hereditary'
gilang	'glittering'
gilang-gemilang	'brilliant, bright'
gunung	'mountain'
gunung-gemunung	'mountain range'
tali	'rope string'
tali-temali	'all kinds of rope, rigging'

If the stem which is reduplicated in this fashion begins with a vowel, the second form is extended by a stop consonant, and the infix is inserted after this consonant; the particular consonant which will be chosen in each particular case is not predictable. (The forms are admittedly uncommon.)

iring	'accompanying'
iring-gemiring	'coming one after another'
ajun	'rock, sway'
ajun-temajun	'rocking to and fro'
aram-temaram	'twilight'

2.2 Bases with Suffixes Only

Bases without prefixes but with suffixes are discussed here. The suffixes -kan and -i do not occur without prefixes except under limited circumstances, namely in the imperative of transitive verbs. These suffixes are accordingly discussed in connection with the prefix meN-. The remaining suffixes occur without prefixes at all, except for the suffix -an which occurs both without any prefix (2.2.1) and also in connection with the prefixes ber- (2.3.3.2), per- (2.6.3), peN- (2.7.4), and ke- (2.8.3, ff.).

2.2.1 The Suffix -an

The suffix -an is used to form nouns from various types of base. (2.2.1.1 to 2.2.1.6). It is also used to form a small number of adjectives and adverbs. (2.2.1.7)

2.2.1.1 When added to a root which can function as a noun, the suffix -an occasionally produces a noun which hardly varies in meaning from the base noun.

ruang	'room'
ruangan	'room'
kelompok	'cluster'
kelompokan	'cluster
empang	'fishpond, dam'
empangan	'fishpond, dam'
simpang	'a branching off'
simpangan	'a branching off'

More usually it produces a noun whose referent has some real or fancied resemblance to the referent of the base noun.

achir	'end'
achiran	'suffix'
anak	'child'
anakan	'interest' (on an investment)
kasih	'affection'
kasihan	'mercy'
ajam	'chicken'
ajam-ajaman	'weathercock'

rambut	'hair'
rambutan	'a fruit' (the 'hairy cherry')
bau	'smell'
bau-bauan	'perfume'
hari	'day'
harian	'daily newspaper'

2.2.1.2 When added to a noun root (usually reduplicated) the suffix -*an* forms a noun which refers to a collection of the referents of the simple noun, or of related referents.

bintang	'star'
bintangan	'constellation'
kaleng	'tin can'
kaleng-kalengan	'canned goods'
pohon	'tree'
pohon-pohonan	'trees, the vegetable kingdom'
daun	'leaf'
dedaunan	'foliage'

2.2.1.3 When added to a numerative (usually only *satu* or those which can be preceded by *satu* in the form *se*-), the suffix -*an* forms a noun referring to a group consisting of that number.

satu	'one'
satuan	'unit'
-puluh	'ten'
puluhan	'decade, a group of ten'
-ratus	'hundred'
ratusan	'a hundred'

-ribu	'thousand'
ribuan	'a thousand'

2.2.1.4 When added to a verb (all other prefixes and suffixes being lost), the suffix -an forms a noun which refers to what is involved in the performance of the action referred to by the verb, whether as the product or the instrument.

makan	'eat'
makanan	'food'
melukis	'draw, paint'
lukisan	'a drawing, a painting'
menggali	'dig'
galian	'what is dug up'
keluar	'emerge'
keluaran	'product'
mengajun	'rock'
ajunan	'cradle'

Such nouns in -an contrast with nouns in ke- -an, per- -an and peN- -an in that they refer to more concrete or definite things, while the three latter groups refer to more abstract processes. Nonetheless, there is sometimes a congruence in meaning between the noun in -an and the other nouns, especially those in per- -an and peN- -an.

harapan	'hope, expectation'
pengharapan	'hope, expectation'
hubungan	'connection'
perhubungan	'connection'
tawaran	'offer, bid, invitation'
penawaran	'offer, bid, bargaining'

tolongan	'help'
pertolongan	'help'

Nouns formed by the addition of <u>per</u>- (extremely rare) and <u>peN</u>- have concrete referents, and there is an occasional overlapping of meanings with the nouns in -<u>an</u>.

penggaris	'ruler, straight-edge'
garisan	'ruler, straight-edge'
pengembus	'bellows'
embusan	'bellows'
pemegang	'handle, holder'
pegangan	'handle'
pengait	'hook, point of attack'
kaitan	'hook, point of attack'

2.2.1.5 Such nouns, derived from verbs by the addition of -<u>an</u>, refer to a collection of items, when the root is reduplicated.

menggali	'dig'
galian	'what is dug up'
gali-galian	'minerals, root crops'
tembak	'shoot'
tembakan	'shot'
tembak-tembakan	'shooting'

2.2.1.6 Just as the suffix -<u>an</u>, added to a reduplicated noun root, produces a noun referring to a collection of items, the same suffix, added to a few adjective roots, usually reduplicated, produces a noun referring to a collection of items which can be characterized by that adjective.

enak	'delicious'
enak-enakan	'delicacies'

asam	'bitter'
asaman	'pickle'
asam-asaman	'all kinds of sour food'
manis	'sweet'
manisan	'candy, sweets'
kotor	'dirty'
kotoran	'trash, litter'

2.2.1.7 Otherwise, adjectives and the occasional verb root, when reduplicated and followed by -an, produce adjectives, or adverbs of manner.

terang	'bright'
terang-terangan	'frank'
merah	'red'
merah-merahan	'reddish'
takut	'afraid'
takut-takutan	'bashful'
hebat	'tremendous'
hebat-hebatan	'on a very large scale'
buta	'blind'
buta-butaan	'at random, blindly'

2.2.2 The suffix -anda is added to certain pronouns and words denoting people, and connotes respect and affection. It thus has a limited distribution and is not freely used to form new words.

anak	'child'
anakanda	'my dear child'
ibu	'mother'
ibunda	'my dear mother'

ajah	'father'
ajahanda	'father'
ajanda	'father'
nenek	'grandfather'
nenekanda	'grandfather'
nenenda	'grandfather'
adik	'younger brother or sister'
adinda	'brother/sister'
kakak	'older brother or sister'
kakanda	'brother/sister'

2.2.3 The suffix -at occurs in words borrowed from Arabic, and is actually an Arabic suffix. A sufficiently large number of words has been borrowed, however, to make the value of the suffix still perceptible in Indonesian. The suffix -at has a limited distribution and is not used to form new words. It derives nouns, usually abstract or generalizing nouns, from various parts of speech.

achir	'end'
achirat	'the hereafter'
hadir	'present'
hadirat	'those present, audience'
maklum	'known'
maklumat	'announcement'

2.2.4 The suffix -i/-wi also occurs in words borrowed from Arabic. The alternant -i occurs after bases ending in a consonant, and the alternant -wi after bases ending in a vowel. The suffix derives adjectives from nouns.

bahadur	'hero'
bahaduri	'heroic'

firdaus	'paradise'
firdausi	'paradisical'
(Isa-al-)Maseh	'Christ'
Masehi	'Christian'
dunia	'world'
duniawi	'worldly'

2.2.5 The suffixes -a and -i occur in words borrowed from Sanskrit and in other words also, by analogy. When they are in direct contrast, -a refers to a male person, -i to a female person. Otherwise, the form in -a refers to both male and female persons.

putera	'prince, son'
puteri	'princess, daughter'
saudara	'gentleman, Mr.'
saudari	'lady, Mrs.'

2.2.6 The suffixes -man/-wan, and -wati similarly occur in words borrowed from Sanskrit. In Sanskrit, -man and -wan form adjectives, which can also be used as nouns, and which are masculine; -wati forms corresponding feminines. In Indonesian, the suffixes -wan and -man are in complementary distribution, with -wan being added to bases which end in a, and -man to other bases; these forms refer to either male or female persons unless they are in direct contrast to a form in -wati, in which case they refer specifically to males. The suffix -wati is added to various bases including those not ending in -a; it refers specifically to females. This is one of the few cases in Indonesian where an affix specifies a distinction between male and female, another being the case of the suffixes -a and -i, just discussed (2.2.5).

mulia	'noble'
muliawan	'a noble'

sastera	'literature'
sasterawan	'man of letters'
warta	'report'
wartawan	'reporter, journalist'
derma	'alms'
dermawan	'charitable'
seni	'art'
seniman	'artist'
seniwati	'female artist'

These suffixes are not true Indonesian suffixes, and are not commonly used in forming new words. One new formation which became common at the time of the crisis over Irian Barat (Western New Guinea) is _sukarelawati_ 'a female volunteer', as opposed to _sukarelawan_, which designates a male volunteer, and _sukarela_, which designates a volunteer in general. Other formations which seem to be recent are:

dutawati	'ambassadress'
(duta	'ambassador')
suarawati	'songstress, female vocalist'
(suara	'voice')
olahragawan	'athlete'
(olahraga	'sport')
peragawati	'mannequin'
(peraga	'show-off')
gamawan	'student from <u>Ga</u>djah <u>Ma</u>da University'

2.3.0 The prefix _ber-_

The prefix _ber-_ occurs with nominal bases (2.3.1); these cases include its occurrence with nominal constructs and the suffix -<u>kan</u> (2.3.1.4). It occurs with numeratives (2.3.2). It also occurs with verbal bases (2.3.3).

2.3.1 The prefix <u>ber</u>- with nouns

The prefix <u>ber</u>- combines with nouns to form predicatives which may be either verbs or adjectives. All such forms are characteristically intransitive.

2.3.1.1 Such a predicate, consisting of <u>ber</u>- and a noun base only, refers to customary possession of, or to characterization by, the referent of the noun.

beranak	'having children'
berkaki	'having feet'
bermaksud	'having an intention'
bersepatu	'wearing shoes'
berperang	'in a state of war'
berpendat	'having an opinion'
berpengetahuan	'having knowledge, scholarly'
bersetudjuan	'having one purpose'
berkehendak	'having a wish'
berkedudukan	'having a residence'
beraliran	'having a tendency'
beruang	'having money, being characterized by the possession of money, monied'
berbagai-bagai	'of differing kinds, manifold'
berbintang-bintang	'having many stars'

Such a predicate may also refer to producing the referent of the noun.

bertelur	'lay an egg'
beranak	'give birth to a child'
berpidato	'make a speech'

berdusta	'tell falsehoods'
berkokok	'produce a cackle'

It may refer to making use of the referent of the noun.

bersepeda	'using a bicycle'
bermalam	'taking advantage of the night'
bertopi	'wearing a hat'
berauto	'travel by car'
berkereta api	'travel by train'

If the noun refers to a title or form of address for a human being, the predicative refers to using that title as a form of address.

tuan	'Mister'
bertuan	'use Mister in addressing a person'

Again, if the noun refers to the profession or way of life of an animate being, the predicative refers to making a living at that profession or by that way of life.

berkuli	'work as a coolie'
bertukang	'work as an artisan'

Occasionally the noun may not refer to an animate being.

bersawah	'work in a rice field'

2.3.1.2 The prefix <u>ber</u>- is added to nouns which are syntactically combined with other words in a nominal structure. These complex structures are thus combined into inseparable morphological compounds, between the elements of which no other morphological or syntactic elements intervene. In the orthography, however, these compounds are written as separate words, the prefix being joined to the first, and so the essential unity of the structure is obscured.

The noun may be modified by an adjective.

kaki pandjang	'long legs'
berkaki pandjang	'long-legged'
badju biru	'blue shirt'
berbadju biru	'wearing a blue shirt'

The noun may be premodified by a numeral. In this case the syntactic order of numeral plus noun is reversed, and the prefix is affixed to the noun, which now occurs in prior place.

empat kaki	'four legs'
berkaki empat	'four-legged'

2.3.1.3 The noun may also form the subject of a sentence structure in which the predicate is a noun-head construction. In this case, the noun which serves as the subject is unmodified in any way, while the noun forming the predicate is rarely modified, though it may be. The resultant construction looks very much like a verb governing an object, because its constituents are written as separate words in the orthography, but again the syntactic inseparability of the constituents shows that the structure is morphologically a unit.

(Botol itu, isinja air.
'That bottle, its contents are water.')

Botol itu berisi air.
"That bottle contains water.'

Botol itu berisi air soda.
'That bottle contains soda water.'

Boto itu berisi air panas.
"That bottle contains hot water.'

Botol itu berisi tiga litar minjak tanah.
'That bottle contains three liters of kerosene.'

2.3.1.4 The Prefix ber- with a Noun Root and the Suffix -kan

In a number of cases where the prefix ber- combines with a sentence structure as described above, the noun which forms the subject of that structure receives the suffix -kan also.

Botol itu berisikan air.
'That bottle contains water.'

Kain itu bertepikan merah.
'The cloth is edged with red.'

Negeri Indonesia berazaskan ketuhanan.
'The Indonesian nation is based on belief in God.'

2.3.2 The Prefix ber- with Numerals

The prefix ber- combines with numerals and numeral-like nouns to make distributives. The combination of ber- with an unreduplicated numeral has the meaning forming a group of.

satu	'one'
bersatu	'united'
dua	'two'
berdua	'two together'
tiga	'three'
bertiga	'three together, in a set of three'

The combination of ber- with a reduplicated numeral has the meaning of in groups of.

ratus	'hundred'
beratus-ratus	'in hundreds'

ribu	'thousand'
beribu-ribu	'in thousands'
tumpuk	'heap, group'
bertumpuk-tumpuk	'in groups, in heaps'
timbun	'heap, pile'
bertimbun-timbun	'in heaps, in piles'
karung	'sack'
berkarung-karung	'in sackfuls'

2.3.3 The Prefix *ber-* with Verbal Bases

The prefix *ber-* combines with verb bases to form intransitive verbs. Bases which do not usually occur without affixes have their general meaning indicated in parentheses.

2.3.3.1 Such verbs may be simply intransitive.

henti	(stop)
berhenti	'come to a stop'
pikir	(think)
berpikir	'be cogitating'
baring	(lie)
berbaring	'be lying down'

If the verb root is reduplicated, there is the additional meaning of variety, repetition or lack of a specific purpose.

djalan	(go, walk)
berdjalan	'walk'
berdjalan-djalan	'go for a stroll'
belit	(twist)
berbelit	'to twist'
berbelit-belit	'to meander'

tjakap	(talk)
bertjakap	'converse'
bertjakap-tjakap	'have a chat'

Such verbs may also be reflexive, that is, the action may be directed at the actor himself.

hias	(adorn)
berhias	'adorn oneself'
tjukur	(trim hair)
bertjukur	'shave oneself'
dandan	(dress)
berdandan	'get dressed'

They may also be reciprocal, that is, there is more than one actor and the action is directed by each at the others.

kelahi	'quarrel'
berkelahi	'quarrel with each other'
gumul	'wrestle'
bergumul	'wrestle with each other'

2.3.3.2 The Prefix ber- with a Verb Root and the Suffix -an

The addition of the suffix -an adds a meaning of reciprocity or variety.

saing	'compete'
bersaingan	'compete with each other'
terbang	'fly'
berterbangan	'fly about in all directions'

hambur	'trickle, spread'
berhamburan	'spread about everywhere'

Compounds also occur.

kirim	'send'
surat	'letter'
berkiriman surat	'maintain a correspondence'

The reduplication of the verb root adds the meaning of multiplicity, variety, or randomness.

pukul	'strike'
berpukul-pukulan	'strike each other repeatedly'
kirim	'send'
surat	'letter'
berkirim-kiriman surat	'send letters back and forth'
lari	'run'
berlari-larian	'run about pointlessly, flock from all directions'

2.3.3.3 The Prefix ber with Syntactically Complex Verbal Bases

The prefix ber- is also added to verb roots which are in some syntactic relationship (usually verb and object) with a noun. These complex structures are thus combined into inseparable morphological compounds, between the elements of which no other morphological or syntactic elements intervene. In the orthography, however, these compounds are written as separate words, the prefix being joined to the verb root, which stands first. Thus the essential unity of the structure is obscured, and so is the fact that the structure is inherently intransitive. From the root tanam 'to plant' and the noun padi 'rice', a compound verb bertanam padi is formed. Such a formation does not mean 'to plant rice'; this would be expressed by the use of a transitive verb plus an object as in menanam padi 'to plant rice'. The meaning of bertanam padi is 'to make a living by planting rice'. Other similar compounds are the following:

djual	'sell'
kuda	'horse'
berdjual kuda	'be a horsetrader'
djual	'sell'
beli	'buy'
berdjual-beli	'make a living by buying and selling'
tenum	'weave'
kain	'cloth'
bertenum kain	'make a living by weaving cloth'
main	'play'
sepak bola	'football'
bermain sepak bola	'play football'

Similar compounds may indicate reciprocity.

tukar	'exchange'
tjintjin	'ring'
bertukar tjintjin	'exchange rings'
kirim	'send'
surat	'letter'
berkirim surat	'exchange letters, correspond'

2.4 The Prefixes meN- and di-

The prefix meN- forms verbs, which may be either transitive or intransitive. (Transitive verbs will be distinguished, when necessary, both

in the Indonesian forms and in the English glosses by the use of the symbol (O) after the verb. Similarly, the symbol (Ø) will be used to indicate that a verb is intransitive when such an indication becomes necessary.) The characteristic of verbs of this type is that they emphasize the actor rather than the action or its object.

All transitive verbs formed with meN- have a corresponding form in which meN- is replaced by di-. The di- form emphasizes the action or the object of the action rather than the actor. The two forms are usually described as being respectively active (the meN- form) and passive (the di- form). In the di- form, all of the other affixes found in the meN- form are preserved.

pukul	(strike)
memukul	'strike (O)'
dipukul	'be struck'
datang	'arrive'
mendatangkan	'import (O)'
didatangkan	'be imported'
air	'water'
mengairi	'irrigate (O)'
diairi	'be irrigated'
tuan	'master'
mempertuan	'accept (O) as master'
dipertuan	'be accepted as master'
baik	'good'
memperbaiki	'repair (O)'
diperbaiki	'be repaired'

An exception must be noted in those cases where a monosyllabic root is made disyllabic by the addition of the vowel e in the transitive; in the passive this vowel does not occur.

tjap	'stamp, seal'
mengetjapkan	'stamp (O)'
ditjapkan	'be stamped'
pak	'pack'
mengepak	'pack (O)'
dipak	'be packed'

Since the chief difference between the forms with meN- and those with di- lies in the syntactic structures into which they enter, a more complete discussion of these differences will be found in the section on syntax. In the ensuing discussion all forms with meN- which are noted as transitive can be assumed to have a corresponding form with di-.

Reduplicated bases also occur with the prefix meN-.

If the prefix is attached to the first member of the reduplication, it is also attached to the second member, according to the description given in 2.0.2.2. The value of the prefix in this case is the same as its value with unreduplicated roots. Examples are to be found in 2.4.1 and the following sections.

If the prefix is attached to the second member of the reduplication only, the result is an intransitive verb with connotations of reciprocality among the actors, or of variety of kinds of action. The reduplicated form may be a base of any type.

a) Noun base

bahu	'shoulder'
bahu-membahu	'work shoulder to shoulder'
dendam	'vengeance'
dendam-mendendam	'hate one another'

b) Verb base

kenal	'be acquainted'
kenal-mengenal	'get acquainted'
tolong	'help'
tolong-menolong	'help each other'
tulis	'write'
tulis-menulis	'write to each other'

c) Adjective base

sedang	'sufficient'
sedang-menjedang	'barely sufficient'

Such forms are also used, without further morphological additions, as nominals.

memasak	'cook (O)'
masak-memasak	'cookery'
mendjahit	'sew (O)'
djahit-mendjahit	'embroidery'
mengarang	'compose (O)'
karang-mengarang	'art of composing'

2.4.1 The Prefix meN- with Nouns

When the prefix meN- is prefixed to nouns, it forms a verb which refers to the use or exploitation of the referent of the noun.

Such verbs are intransitive, for the most part.

tari	'a dance'
menari	'to dance'
pekik	'a scream'
memekik	'to utter a scream'

keluh	'sigh, complaint'
mengeluh	'to sigh, complain'
uak	'lowing'
menguak	'to low'
darat	'terra firma'
mendarat	'to land, go ashore'
seberang	'the other side'
menjeberang	'to go to the other side'
rotan	'rattan'
merotan	'to gather rattan'
damar	'resin'
mendamar	'to gather resin'
sajur	'vegetables'
menjajur	'to make vegetable soup'
tari	'dance'
menari-nari	'cavort, jump for joy'
tingkat	'level'
meningkat-ningkat	'increase, rise'

But some are transitive.

gergadji	'saw'
menggergadji	'to saw (O)'
kapur	'chalk, whitewash'
mengapur	'to whitewash (O)'
sapu	'broom'
menjapu	'to sweep (O)'

2.4.2 The Prefix meN- with Numeratives

When prefixed to numeratives, the prefix meN- forms intransitive verbs.

dua	'two'
mendua	'become two, to be twofold'
Hatinja mendua.	'He is of two minds. (His mind is twofold.)'
tiga	'three'
meniga	'to be threefold'

Such forms are extremely rare, however, except for mendua.

When prefixed to certain numerals modifying the noun hari 'day', a compound verb is formed which refers to observing the ceremonial which is set for a fixed day after a person's death.

tiga hari	'three days'
Mereka meniga hari datuknja.	'They are observing the ceremonial for the third day after their grandfather's death.'

2.4.3 The Prefix meN- with Verb Bases

2.4.3.1 When prefixed to verb bases, the prefix meN- forms both transitive and intransitive verbs. Verb bases which do not usually occur without affixes have their general meaning given in parentheses.

Most such verbs are transitive.

lihat	(see)
melihat	'look at (O)'

tunggu	(wait)
menunggu	'wait for (O)'
antjam	(threaten)
mengantjam	'to threaten (O)'
balik	(be upside down, be wrong side to)
membalik	'to turn (O), to change (O)'
dengar	(listen)
mendengar	'hear (O)'
buka	(open)
membuka	'to open (O)'
tulis	(write)
menulis	'write (O)'

2.4.3.1 Others are intransitive.

rebah	(fall, lie)
merebah	'fall down'
rontok	(fall of leaves)
merontok	'fall' (of leaves)
turun	'go down, descend'
menurun	'go down, decline'
datang	'arrive'
mendatang	'come in due order'
djadi	'become'
mendjadi-djadi	'increase, grow greater'

2.4.4 The Prefix meN- with Adjectives

When prefixed to adjectives, the prefix meN- forms verbs which are generally intransitive.

merah	'red'
memerah	'to turn red'
tipis	'thin'
menipis	'to become thin'
gelap	'dark'
menggelap	'to become dark'
hitam	'black'
menghitam	'to become black'
kanan	'right'
menganan	'to move to the right'
tinggi	'high'
meninggi	'to rise'

2.4.5 The Affixations meN- -kan and meN- -i

The suffixes -kan and -i are added to bases which also have the prefix meN-; all such verbs (except mendjadikan 'become') are transitive.

The relationship of a verb which has the suffix to the corresponding verb which does not have the suffix is as follows.

2.4.5.1 If the verb without the suffix is transitive, the verb with the suffix may occasionally be indistinguishable from it in meaning. The suffix in this case is usually -kan, rarely -i.

mengalih	'change (O)'
mengalihkan	'change (O)'
memetjah	'analyse (O)'
memetjahkan	'analyse (O)'
menghormat	'honor (O)'
menghormati	'honor (O)'

melabuh	'drop (anchor, foal)'
melabuhkan	'drop (anchor, foal)'
menjusup	'crawl under (O)'
menjusupi	'crawl under (O)'

2.4.5.2 If the verb without the suffix is transitive, and the verb with the suffix differs in meaning, it usually differs in one or more of the following ways.

a) The suffix -kan is benefactive, indicating that the action of the verb is performed for someone else, as a favor to him. Such a verb can be doubly transitive, having as its primary object (Op) a noun which could occur as the object of the verb without the suffix -kan, and having as its secondary object (Os) a noun referring to the person in whose stead or on whose behalf the action is performed. When both objects follow the verb, and neither is governed by a preposition, the secondary object precedes the primary object.

membeli (Op)	'buy (Op)'
membelikan (Os) (Op)	'buy (Op) as a favor to (Os)'

Dia membelikan saja buku itu.
'He bought me that book (and so saved me from having to go to the bookstore).'

membatja (Op)	'read (Op)'
membatjakan (Os) (Op)	'read (Op) instead of (Os)'

Dia membatjakan saja surat itu.
'He read me that letter (because I didn't have my glasses).'

mentjutji (Op)	'launder (Op)'
mentjutjikan (Os) (Op)	'launder (Op) for (Os)'

Dia mentjutjikan saja badju ini.
'She washed this shirt for me.'

The secondary object can be replaced by a prepositional phrase consisting of a preposition (either untuk or buat) and the noun which serves as the secondary object. Such a prepositional phrase follows the primary object when both follow the verb.

Dia membelikan buku itu untuk saja.
Dia membatjakan surat itu buat saja.
Dia mentjutjikan badju ini buat saja.

b) The suffix -kan is directive with verbs implying direction, indicating that the action of the verb is directed at a specific person. Such a verb can also be doubly transitive, having as its primary object (Op) the noun which could occur as the object of the verb without the suffix -kan, and having as its secondary object (Os) a noun referring to the person towards whom the action is directed. When both objects follow the verb, and neither is governed by a preposition, the secondary object precedes the primary object.

memberi (Op) 'give (Op)'
memberikan (Os) (Op) 'give (Os) (Op)'
Dia memberikan saja buku itu.
'He gave me that book.'

mengirim (Op) 'send (Op)'
mengirimkan (Op) (Op) 'send (Op) to (Os)'
Dia mengirimkan Ali uang itu.
'He sent that money to Ali.'

The secondary object can be, and indeed usually is, replaced by a prepositional phrase consisting of the preposition kepada and the noun which serves as the secondary object. Such a prepositional phrase follows the primary object when both follow the verb.

Dia memberikan buku itu kepada saja.
Dia mengirim uang itu kepada Ali.

2.4.5.3 The suffix -kan may also be causative, indicating that the object is caused to perform the action by someone else.

menjusul	'follow (O)'
menjusulkan	'append (O), send (O) after, cause (O) to follow'
menjewa	'rent (O)'
menjewakan	'lease (O), cause (O) to be rented'

2.4.5.4 The suffix -i may be iterative, indicating that the action of the verb is performed repeatedly.

memukul	'strike (O)'
memukuli	'strike (O) repeatedly'
mengangkat	'remove (O)'
mengangkati	'remove (a number of things)'
menggambar	'make a picture of (O)'
menggambari	'illustrate (a book)'

2.4.5.5 The suffix -i may also be allative, indicating that the action of the verb moves toward or onto the object of the verb, or is directed toward or onto it, or is applied to it.

mengadjar	'teach (O) (algebra)'
mengadjari	'teach to (O) (students)
menulis	'write (O) (a sentence)'
menulisi	'write on (O) (the blackboard)'
memakan	'eat (O) (fruit)'
memakani	'bring food to (O) (children)'

melempar	'throw (O) (stones)'
melempari	'throw things at (O) (the house)'

2.4.6 If the verb without the suffix is intransitive, the verb with the suffix is transitive in one of the following ways.

2.4.6.1 The suffix -kan has a causative effect, indicating that the subject causes the object to perform the action referred to by the verb without the suffix.

a) From nouns:

darat	'dry land'
mendarat	'go ashore'
mendaratkan	'put (O) ashore'
seberang	'opposite side'
menjeberang	'cross to the opposite side'
menjeberangkan	'take (O) across'
taksi	'taxi'
menaksi	'drive a taxi'
menaksikan	'make (O) into a taxi'
hilir	'downstream'
menghilir	'float downstream'
menghilirkan	'let (O) drift with the stream'

b) From verbs:

merebah	'fall down'
merebahkan	'knock (O) over'
merontok	'fall (of leaves)'
merontokkan	'cause (leaves) to fall'

menjuruk	'duck, hide'
menjurukkan	'duck (the head), hide (O)'
menurun	'go down, decline'
menurunkan	'cause (O) to decline'
mendatang	'arrive'
mendatangkan	'cause (O) to arrive'

c) From adjectives:

tinggi	'high'
meninggi	'rise'
meninggikan	'raise (O)'
tipis	'thin'
menipis	'become thin'
menipiskan	'make (O) thin'
merah	'red'
memerah	'become red'
memerahkan	'cause (O) to become red'
kiri	'left'
mengiri	'keep to the left'
mengirikan	'move (O) to the left'

2.4.7 If the verb without the suffix does not occur, then the verb with the suffix is simply transitive.

mengabaikan	'ignore (O)'
membabarkan	'spread (O)'
mendahului	'be ahead of (O)
mendahulukan	'give precedence to (O)'
menggerumuti	'swarm about (O)'
menjelang-njelingkan	'vary (O)'
mengata-ngatai	'scold (O), tease (O)'

2.4.8 When the suffixes -kan and -i are in direct contrast with each other, the difference in meaning is usually the following:

The suffix -kan denotes that the referent of the object is caused to undergo the process referred to by the underlying forms. If the verb with -kan is based on a verbal root, then the object is caused to perform the action referred to by that root. If the verb with -kan is based on an adjectival root, the object is caused to adopt the characteristic referred to by that adjective. If the verb with -kan is based on a noun root, then the object is usually caused to become the referent of that noun.

The suffix -i denotes that the referent of the subject is applied to, approaches, or is caused to approach the referent of the object of the verb. If the root of the verb is a noun root, then the referent of that noun may be applied to the object.

darat	'dry land'
mendarat	'come to land'
mendaratkan	'bring (O) to land'
mendarati	'land on (O)'
datang	'arrive'
mendatangkan	'cause (O) to arrive, bring (O)'
mendatangi	'arrive at (O), visit (O)'
dekat	'close'
mendekat	'approach'
mendekatkan	'cause (O) to approach'
mendekati	'approach (O)'
singgah	'stop by, visit'
menjinggahkan	'cause (O) to stop'
menjinggahi	'stop at (O)'

minjak	'oil'
meminjaki	'oil (O)'

2.4.9 The Prefix memper-

The prefix memper- is structurally the prefix meN- plus the prefix per-, with an anomalous retention of the initial p- of per- when the prefix meN- is added. The prefix meN- in this combination is replaced in the passive and in the imperative in the same way as in other transitive verbs in which it occurs.

The meaning of this combination of prefixes is, however, not described here as the sum of a particular meaning of meN- plus a particular meaning of per-; as far as meaning is concerned, the combination is most easily described as a unit.

The combined prefix memper- makes transitive verbs which can generally be described as causative; causative verbs are also made with the prefix meN- and the suffix -kan. It is sometimes stated that there is a difference between these two types of causative verb such that, from

tinggi	'high'

two different verbs are said to be derived:

meninggikan	'to raise (something which was low)'
mempertinggi	'to raise higher (something which was already high)'

This distinction is not always observed by most speakers, who generally regard the forms as essentially the same. In addition, there is a considerable number of pairs of verbs, one of which has the complex prefix memper- and the other of which has the prefix meN- and the suffix -kan, with no distinction in meaning between the two, or with distinctions of a different kind. There are also a number of verbs which have both the complex prefix <u>memper</u>- and the suffix -<u>kan</u>. All such verbs are causative. They are derived from adjectives, from nouns, and occasionally from other verbs.

There are verbs which have the prefix <u>memper</u>- and the suffix -<u>i</u>, in which the prefix does not seem to have any more effect than the prefix <u>meN</u>- alone.

tuan	'master'
mempertuan	'treat (O) as a master'
besar	'big, great'
membesarkan	'make (O) great'
memperbesar	'make (O) big'
memperbesarkan	'make (O) big'
baik	'good'
membaiki	'play up to (O)'
membaikkan	'make (O) good'
memperbaiki	'correct (O), repair (O)'
tukar	'change'
mempertukarkan	'exchange (O)'
menukarkan	'exchange (O)'
tjerai	'part'
mempertjeraikan	'separate (O)'
mentjeraikan	'separate (O)'
kuat	'strong'
memperkuat	'lend support to (O)'
menguatkan	'strengthen (O), corroborate (O)'
menguati	'coerce (O); lend support to (O)'

ketjil	'small'
memperketjil	'make (O) small'
mengetjilkan	'make (O) small'

2.5 The Prefix ter-

2.5.1 The Prefix ter- with Verbs

The prefix ter- is used to form deverbal adjectives in which the emphasis is on the action, and in which the agent is usually unimportant, non-existent, or so general as to be virtually non-existent.

2.5.1.1 The prefix ter- replaces the prefix meN- in a transitive verb to form a deverbal adjective with a passive sense; such passive constructions are usually unaccompanied by any reference to the performer of the action.

membuka	'open (O)'
terbuka	'opened'
melihat	'see (O)'
terlihat	'seen'
menulis	'write (O)'
tertulis	'written'
memutus	'break (O)'
terputus	'broken'

When the prefix ter- replaces the prefix meN- of a verb which also has the suffix -kan or the suffix -i, this suffix is ordinarily lost. Occasionally, however, the suffix is retained. The retention may be useful, to some speakers, in distinguishing the form derived from a transitive verb with a suffix from a form derived from an intransitive verb without the suffix; however, the forms without suffixes, though listed in certain dictionaries, are rare.

(melampau)	(go too far)
(terlampau)	(accidentally go too far)
melampaui	'(pass (O), skip (O)'
terlampaui	'passed, skipped'
mengatakan	'describe, talk about'
tidak terkatakan	'indescribable'
menjelami	'study (O)'
terselami	'well-understood'

2.5.1.2 This prefix also replaces the prefixes meN- or ber- in intransitive verbs to form a deverbal adjective or a deverbal verb. Such forms are necessarily not passive in meaning. They generally include a connotation of lack of control, or of being the victim of circumstances.

melajang	'fly, soar'
terlajang	'float, wander (aimlessly)'
berbatuk	'cough'
terbatuk-batuk	'cough repeatedly (uncontrollably)'
bergesa-gesa	'hurry intentionally'
tergesa-gesa	'hurry because driven'
mengesak	'sob'
teresak-esak	'burst out in sobs'

2.5.1.3 There are also formations with the prefix ter- which are not related directly to existing verb forms. Such forms are uncommon.

tergegan	'shocked with fright'
tergelebar	'flap (in the wind)'
terkehel	'off course'
terkelap, tekerlap	'dozed off'
terlena	'be unable to keep awake'

2.5.1.4 The prefix ter- includes the implication that an action is accidental and so not performed intentionally by any agent.

meninggalkan	'leave (O) behind'
tertinggal	'be accidentally left behind'
membawa	'take (O)'
terbawa	'be taken by mistake'
memakan	'eat (O)'
termakan	'to be eaten by mistake'
melipat	'fold (O), crease'
terlipat	'get creased by accident'
memidjat	'step on (O)'
terpidjat	'get stepped on by accident'

2.5.1.5 The prefix ter- also implies that the action of the basic verb is able to be performed in general, and by any agent. This particular usage occurs most frequently with the negative tidak.

membatja	'read'
tidak terbatja	'not able to be read'
mendengar	'hear'
terdengar	'audible'
mengangkat	'lift'
terangkat	'capable of being lifted'

2.5.1.6 In cases where the agent is specified, (though this is uncommon), the preposition oleh is used to mark the agent.

tertulis oleh orang lama	'written by the people of old'
terambil oleh ibu	'accidentally taken by mother'
terangkat oleh saja	'capable of being lifted by me'

2.5.2 The Prefix _ter_- with Adjectives

The prefix _ter_- is added to adjectives to make the superlative.

besar	'big'
terbesar	'extremely big, biggest'
tinggi	'high'
tertinggi	'highest'
bagus	'beautiful'
terbagus	'most beautiful'

However, _ter_- is not used with adjectives prefixed with _ber_-. The form _paling_ is preposed instead.

berguna	'useful'
paling berguna	'most useful'

The form _paling_ may also be used with other adjectives, in place of _ter_-.

besar	'big'
paling besar	'biggest'

2.6 The Prefix _per_-

2.6.1 The prefix _per_- replaces the prefix _ber_- of verbs and adjectives, and so forms a noun indicating the person or instrument performing the action referred to by that verb, or possessing the quality referred to by that adjective. There are very few incontestable examples of this formation, however. (See Section 2.7).

tapa	(asceticism)
bertapa	'characterized by asceticism'
pertapa	'ascetic'
adjar	'study'
beladjar	'devoted to study'
peladjar	'student'

2.6.2 The prefix <u>per-</u> is attached to numerals to form fractions; such fractions function as nouns.

dua	'two'
perdua	'half'
tiga	'three'
pertiga	'third'
dua pertiga	'two-thirds'
empat	'four'
perempat	'fourth'
seperempat	'one fourth'
tiga perempat	'three fourths'

2.6.3 <u>per- -an</u>

In a few cases, the prefix <u>per-</u> replaces the prefix <u>ber-</u> in verbs, and combines with the suffix <u>-an</u> to form nouns referring to the process of action referred to by the verb. Occasionally the noun refers to the place where the action is performed.

tapa	'asceticism'
bertapa	'characterized by asceticism'
pertapa	'ascetic'
pertapaan	'asceticism, hermitage'
adjar	'study'
beladjar	'devoted to study'

peladjar	'student'
peladjaran	'studying, lesson'

More frequently, the per- -an combination forms nouns irrespective of any underlying form with ber-. Such forms sometimes contrast with, and sometimes freely alternate with nouns formed with the combination peN- -an. (See Section 2.7.4).

tjoba	'try'
pertjobaan	'result of trying, trial'
satu	'one'
bersatu	'characterized by oneness, united'
persatuan	'state of being a unit, unity, union'

2.7 The Prefix peN-

2.7.1 The prefix peN- replaces the prefix meN- in verbs, the suffixes -kan and -i being omitted also, to form a noun indicating the person or instrument which performs the action referred to by that verb. In contemporary Indonesian, a strict distinction between the prefixes per- and peN- is not generally maintained except in a few cases where there is a clear contrast between two verbs formed of the same root, one with the prefix ber-, and the other with the prefix meN-. In cases where such a clearcut distinction is not made, the verb may occur with one or the other of the two verbal prefixes, and the corresponding noun occurs with one or the other of the noun prefixes, without any strict parallelism between ber- and per- and between meN- and peN-. On the whole, formations with per- are decidedly few in number as compared with those with peN-.

menulis	'write (O)'
penulis	'writer'

mengadjar	'teach (O)'
pengadjar	'teacher'

2.7.2 The prefix <u>peN-</u> appears to occur with nouns to indicate a person who makes use of the referent of that noun, but such formations are usually derivable through a verb form.

madat	'opium'
memadat	'to smoke opium'
pemadat	'opium smoker'
kopi	'coffee'
mengopi	'to drink coffee'
pengopi	'coffee hound'
laut	'sea'
pelaut	'sailor'

2.7.3 The prefix <u>peN-</u> occurs with adjectives to form nouns which indicate a person who can be characterized by the referent of that adjective.

muda	'young'	pemuda	'a youth'
malas	'lazy'	pemalas	'lazybones'
besar	'big'	pembesar	'a big shot, principal'

2.7.4 The prefix <u>peN-</u> replaces the prefix <u>meN-</u> in verbs, and, in combination with the suffix <u>-an</u>, forms a noun referring to the act of performing the action referred to by the verb. The noun thus denotes the active transitive process of the verb, and stands, on occasion, in direct contrast with the noun in which the prefix <u>ke-</u> and the suffix <u>-an</u> occur, which denotes the end-result of the action referred to by the verb. (See Sections 2.8.3.1 and 2.6.3.)

mendidik	'educate'
pendidik	'educator'
pendidikan	'education, pedagogy'

mengadjar	'teach'
pengadjar	'teacher'
pengadjaran	'instruction'
mentjoba	'try'
pentjobaan	'act of trying, trial'
satu	'one'
menjatu	'unify'
penjatuan	'act of unifying, unification, union'

2.8 The Prefix ke-

This prefix is seldom used, except in conjunction with the suffix -an. The combination ke- -an as a noun-formant is, however, one of the most productive in the language.

2.8.1 The prefix ke- is used with a restricted number of other forms to form nouns.

tua	'old
ketua	'elder, chairman'
hendak	'wish, want'
kehendak	'will, desire'
kasih	'affection'
kekasih	'darling'

(In this last case, it is possible that kekasih represents a partial reduplication of the kind found in lelaki for laki-laki.)

2.8.2 The prefix ke- is used with numerals to form ordinal adjectives and collective numerals. (See Section 3.1.3.4).

tiga	'three'
ketiga	'third'
ketiga	'three(some)'

seki	'so much'
sekian	'such and such'
kesekian	'umpteenth, nth'

2.8.3 ke- -an Forming Nouns

The prefix ke- in combination with the suffix -an forms nouns from verbs and adjectives, and occasionally from other form-classes.

In the course of this formation, the suffixes -kan and -i are lost upon the addition of the suffix -an; any prefixes are usually lost upon the addition of the prefix ke- (certain exceptions to this latter statement will be given in the examples).

2.8.3.1 Nouns thus formed from verbs refer to the end result of the action of the verb. When they contrast with nouns formed only by the addition of the suffix -an, the form with -an is generally more concrete, and the form with ke- and -an is generally more abstract. When they contrast with nouns formed by the addition of the prefix peN- or per- and the suffix -an, the latter forms refer to the process of the action of the verb, and the former, as mentioned above, refer to the end result of that action. Nouns formed from adjectives refer to the quality, color, etc., referred to by the adjective.

besar	'big'
membesarkan	'make big'
kebesaran	'bigness'
ada	'exist'
mengadakan	'organize, create'
keadaan	'existence'
ahli	'expert'
keahlian	'expertness'

bangun	'arise'
kebangunan	'awakening'
satu	'one'
menjatu	'unify'
kesatuan	'result of unification, unity'
bisa	'be able'
kebisaan	'capability'
mampu	'be able'
tidak mampu	'not be able'
ketidakmampuan	'impotence'
adil	'just'
tidak adil	'not just'
ketidakadilan	'injustice'

2.8.3.2 The prefix ke- in combination with the suffix -an forms nouns from nouns. The nouns formed in this way are abstract.

Tuhan	'God'	ketuhanan	'godhead'
anggota	'member'	keanggotaan	'membership'
bangsa	'nation, rank'	kebangsaan	'nationality, nobility'
binatang	'animal'	kebinatangan	'bestiality'
daerah	'region'	kedaerahan	'provincial-ism'

2.8.4 ke- -an Forming Verbs

The prefix ke- in combination with the suffix -an forms verbs from different kinds of bases. These verbs generally carry a connotation of performing an action unintentionally or, more frequently, suffering an action by mischance. This type of formation is relatively common in Javanese, and the Indonesian forms may be regarded as Javanese constructions utilizing Indonesian elements. This formation is relatively active in Indonesian, however, and cannot be dismissed as merely a Javanism.

betul	'correct'
kebetulan	'chance to be correct'
air	'water'
keairan	'be flooded'
bakar	'fire'
kebakaran	'catch on fire, be damaged by fire'
mendapat	'find, discover'
kedapatan	'be found out, discovered'
panas	'hot'
kepanasan	'be afflicted by the heat'
hudjan	'rain'
kehudjanan	'be caught in the rain'
malam	'darkness'
kemalaman	'be overtaken by darkness'
tahu	'know'
ketahuan	'come to be known'
lihat	'see'
kelihatan	'be visible'
dengar	'hear'
kedengaran	'be audible'
bandjir	'salt water'
kebandjiran	'be flooded by the sea'

Sometimes the base is a sentence structure consisting of a subject and a predicate; the predicate of this structure is either intransitive or passive. The root of this predicate accepts the prefix _ke-_ and the suffix _-an_, and is followed by the subject of the sentence structure.

Pohon djatuh.	'The tree fell.'
Ia kedjatuhan pohon.	'He was struck by a falling tree.'
Buku hilang.	'The book got lost.'
Saja kehilangan buku.	'I chanced to lose my book.'
Sepeda ditjuri.	'The bicycle was stolen.'
Ali ketjurian sepeda.	'Ali's bicycle has been stolen.'

The combination makes a compound predicative similar in general function to a passive verb. If the agent is to be specified, the preposition _oleh_ occurs.

Ali kelihatan oleh saja.	'Ali chanced to be seen by me.' 'I caught a glimpse of Ali.'

2.8.5 _ke- -an_ Forming Adjectives

2.8.5.1 The prefix _ke-_ in combination with the suffix _-an_ combines with adjectives to form adjectives with a connotation of extremeness or intensity. This formation is borrowed from Javanese but is becoming common, especially in Djakarta.

besar	'big'
kebesaran	'too big, extremely big'
ketjil	'small'
keketjilan	'too small, extremely small'

keras	'hard'
kekerasan	'too hard, extremely hard'

These forms correspond directly to the more typically Indonesian forms terlalu besar, terlalu ketjil, terlalu keras.

Sepatu ini kebesaran.
'These shoes are too big.'
Sepatu ini terlalu besar.
'These shoes are too big.'

2.8.5.2 The prefix ke- and the suffix -an combine with reduplicated roots to form adjectives. Such adjectives imply possessing the characteristics of the root to a certain degree, and frequently to an inadequate degree.

gelap	'dark'
kegelap-gelapan	'dim, dusky'
gila	'crazy'
kegila-gilaan	'half-mad'
heran	'astonished'
keheran-heranan	'dumbfounded'
malu	'shy'
kemalu-maluan	'to be very much ashamed'
ilmu	'science'
keilmu-ilmuan	'quasi-scientific'
hitam	'black'
kehitam-hitaman	'blackish'
anak	'child'
keanak-anakan	'childish'
Belanda	'Dutchman'
keBelanda-Belandaan	'occidentalized'

2.9 The Prefix se-

The prefix se- is a modification of the full word form satu 'one'. In many of the cases discussed here, se- can be replaced by satu, at least in theory; in practice se- is much more common.

2.9.1 The prefix se- occurs as a prefix to nouns for the most part, and with the following meanings.

2.9.1.1 With numeratives and count nouns, the prefix indicates that only one quantity or example is referred to.

sepuluh	'ten'
seratus	'a hundred'
seribu	'one thousand'
seperempat	'one quarter'
seorang dokter	'one doctor'
seekor kuda	'one horse'
sehelai kertas	'one sheet of paper'
sesikat pisang	'one hand of bananas'

2.9.1.2 With other nouns, this prefix forms a predicative with a meaning being the same as, or sharing the same characteristics. Such predicatives usually govern a prepositional construct introduced by the preposition dengan 'with'.

laras	'harmony'
selaras	'in harmony'
padan	'equal, peer'
sepadan	'match, harmonize'
kantor	'office'
sekantor	'work in the same office'

kampung	'village'
sekampung	'hail from the same village'

2.9.1.3 With nouns denoting time periods, the prefix has various meanings. In some cases it has the meanings already discussed.

sewaktu	'at the same time as'
setahun	'one year'

In other cases, additional meanings are also possible.

semalam	'one night' 'last night'

If the root is reduplicated, the connotation of repetition is introduced.

sehari-hari	'daily, everyday'
sewaktu-waktu	'always, at any time'
sekali-kali	'from time to time'
sekali-kali tidak	'never under any circumstances'

Occasionally both prefix and root are reduplicated.

sekali-sekali	'once in a while'

2.9.1.4 With predicatives (adjectives or verbs) the prefix usually forms adverbials of manner.

sekuat	'with all one's strength'
selalu	'continuously'

2.9.1.5 The prefix <u>se</u>- occurs frequently in forms which function as conjunctions. Different kinds of bases occur.

sudah	'finished'
sesudah	'after'
belum	'not yet'
sebelum	'before'

2.9.2 se- -an

When the prefix se- occurs with the suffix -an, two situations are possible. The more usual is that the prefix se- has been added to a noun formed by the addition of the suffix -an.

imbang	'balanced'
imbangan	'a balance, equilibrium'
seimbangan	'in equilibrium'

The other is that prefix and suffix combine, usually with the reduplicated root of a noun denoting a time period, to form an adverbial of time.

sehari-harian	'all day through'
semalam-malaman	'the whole night'

2.9.3 se- -nja

2.9.3.1 The prefix se- and the enclitic -nja combine freely with reduplicated adjective bases to form adverbials of manner.

sebaik-baiknja	'as good as possible'
sebesar-besarnja	'as big as possible'
sebetul-betulnja	'as correct as possible'

A certain number of verb roots also occur.

sedapat-dapatnja	'as much as can be'
semau-maunja	'as much as one wants'
sedjadi-djadinja	'with all one's might'

Other roots also sometimes occur.

setidak-tidaknja	'at very least'

2.9.3.2 The prefix <u>se</u>- and the enclitic -<u>nja</u> combine to form connectives or sentence adverbs.

sebetulnja	'the truth of it is that...' 'truthfully, in truth'
seharusnja	'the obligation in this matter is that...' 'should'
sesudahnja	'finally'
selainnja	'as for the remainder of it'

F O R M - C L A S S E S

3.0 Words

Morphemes combine to form words.

A word in Indonesian consists of a root, of a root with an infix, of a reduplicated root, or of more than one root fused into a compound, along with as many of the immediately preceding morphemes as are prefixes, and as many of the immediately following morphemes as are suffixes.

Just as the phoneme may have alternate forms (allophones) which occur in specific phonemic environments, and the morpheme may have alternate forms (allomorphs) which occur in specific morphological environments, so the word may have alternate forms which occur in specific environments involving other words. (Thus, the word aku 'I' has alternate forms ku- and -ku which occur, respectively, with verb structures and with noun structures.)

Words and their alternate forms are either free, in which case they occur freely in all positions in an utterance, or bound, in which case they occur only in a fixed positional relationship to other words. It is possible for a word to be free in one of its alternate forms (e.g., English not), and bound in another (e.g., English -n't, which can occur only after a restricted number of verb forms in a verb structure).

A bound word, or a bound word-alternant is called a clitic. Clitics may be further distinguished in accordance with the position they occupy when they are joined to a structure. Those which occur before a particular item of the structure are called proclitics. Those which occur after a particular item of the structure are called enclitics. Other types of clitics may be distinguished in language in general, but in the particular case of the Indonesian language, only proclitics and enclitics occur. Thus aku 'I' is a free form. Its alternate form -ku is an enclitic to nominal structures, and its alternate form ku- is a proclitic to certain verb structures.

Indonesian orthography joins some clitics to the word to which they are bound. Proclitics which are joined in this manner are given here followed by a hyphen (ku-, di-, etc.); it is understood that these proclitics are to be written as one word with the following item, unless that item begins with a capital letter, in which case the proclitic is written separately (kubeli, dirumah, di Djakarta). Similarly, enclitics which are joined in this manner are given here preceded by a hyphen (-ku, -nja, etc.); these enclitics are to be written as one word with the preceding item (rumahku, rumahnja). Clitics which are not ordinarily joined to another word in the orthography are given without hyphens.

Words, including clitics, can be assigned to form-classes on the basis of the manner in which they interrelate with other words.

But any attempt to describe these form-classes as classes of single words will encounter difficulty; though the specific function of each class can be fulfilled in cases by a single word, in other cases it is fulfilled by a group of words linked syntactically (a construct). Thus, an adequate description of a form-class will, in many cases, involve a discussion of words and of constructs together.

Many constructs center around one word which can fulfil the same structural function as the entire construct. Such constructs are called endocentric. The central word is called the head of the construct and the construct is called the expansion of that head. For example, an endocentric construct which has a noun head can function exactly like a simple noun. In discussing any form-class, then, it is advisable to discuss also the endocentric constructs in which a member of that form-class can serve as the head.

Other constructs, which are called exocentric, are composed of words from various form-classes in such a way that no word in the construct could serve the same function as the entire construct. For example, an exocentric construct which consists of a preposition and a noun construct can function as an adverb, despite the fact that there may be no adverb in the construct. It will therefore be necessary to discuss such exocentric constructs as members of the form-class whose function they fulfil.

In Indonesian there are three major form-classes. These are the class of nominals, the class of predicatives and the class of adjuncts. Each of these can be subdivided into a number of minor form-classes.

The class of nominals and their expansions is discussed beginning with Section 3.1. The class of predicatives and their expansions is discussed beginning with Section 3.2. The class of adjuncts is discussed beginning with Section 3.3.

3.1 Nominals

The class of nominals is subdivided into a number of subclasses. These are: Pronouns (3.1.1), Nouns (3.1.2), Numeratives (3.1.3), Counter Nouns (3.1.4), Determiners (3.1.5) and Nominalizations (3.1.6). Nominal expansions are discussed in 3.1.7, partial nominal expansions in 3.1.8, and pronominal expansions in 3.1.9.

3.1.1 Pronouns

The pronouns exhibit a variety of forms. This is due in part to the preservation in the pronouns of some of the honorific distinctions which are so common in the Malayo-Polynesian languages in general but which have been otherwise largely lost in contemporary Indonesian. It is therefore advisable to divide the pronouns into three classes, the informal, the formal, and the very formal. This is, however, a loose classification, and must not be insisted upon, since it is likely to change from one speaker to another depending upon his local language.

3.1.1.1 The pronouns are:

Informal	Formal	Very Formal	Equivalent
aku, -ku, ku- gua	saja	saja (hamba) (beta)	'I'
engkau, -kau, kau- kamu, -mu lu	<u>N</u> (anda)	<u>N</u>	'you' (singular)

Informal	Formal	Very Formal	Equivalent
ia, dia, -nja	ia, dia, -nja	beliau	'he, she'
kita	kita	kita	'we' (inclusive)
kami	kami	kami	'we' (exclusive)
kamu, -mu	N (anda)	N	'you' (plural)
mereka, -nja	mereka, -nja	beliau-beliau	'they'

3.1.1.2 The forms which occur only in the Informal column are used in talking to members of one's own family or to very good friends. Otherwise, there may be a connotation of condescension, or even of calculated insult, depending on the parts of the country from which speaker and hearer come. The forms gua 'I' and lu 'you' are informal to the point of rudeness.

The forms which occur in the Formal column are used in polite everyday situations.

The forms which occur in the Very Formal column are used in talking to or about people who are markedly superior in social position, such as, for example, the President of the Republic of Indonesia, or other heads of state. They also tend to be used in formal speeches and other public utterances for referring to officials or auditors, or to well-known personalities.

baru dalam tahun 1912 beliau mendirikan negara baru diatas "Weltanschauung" San Min Chu I itu,

'only in the year 1912 did he (Sun Yat Sen) establish a new state on the basis of his philosophical outlook, "The Three Principles of the People".'

3.1.1.3 The enclitic forms of the pronouns, marked in the list by being written with a hyphen before them, are used chiefly with nouns or noun constructs to denote possession.

buku	'book'
bukuku	'my book'
bukukau	'your book'
bukumu	'your books'
bukunja	'his book', 'her book', or 'their books'
buku biruku	'my blue book'

All of these suffixes are only informal except -nja, which is informal and possibly formal.

The enclitic -nja, in addition to having the usage and meaning described here, is also used as a nominalizing enclitic (see Section 3.1.6), as well as for relating the topic to the subject of the comment in topic-comment sentences (see Section 4.7).

3.1.1.4 The proclitic forms of the pronouns, marked in the above list by being written with a hyphen after them, are used with passive verbs to denote the agent.

membeli	'to buy (O)'
dibeli	'to be bought'
Ali beli	'bought by Ali'
kubeli	'bought by me'
kaubeli	'bought by you'

These proclitic forms, especially _ku-_, are less informal than the enclitic forms, and may occur even at a very formal level of speaking or writing, without any connotation of intimacy, condescension or insult.

3.1.1.5 The pronouns _ia_ and _dia_ are used in referring to persons of either sex. _Dia_ is the more frequent. Some speakers use it exclusively in cases where there is a contrast between pronouns, as in

Ia pergi.	'He went.'
Saja pergi; dia tidak.	'I went; he didn't.'

There is in general no pronoun which can be used to refer to animals or things. Either no form occurs, or the noun is repeated.

Kuda itu, kuda saja. Kuda itu kuat.
or
Kuda itu, kuda saja. Kuat.
'That horse is mine. It's strong.'

However, _dia_ is commonly found in referring to inanimates in the sentences.

Ini dia.	'This is it.'
Itu dia.	'That is it.'

Examples are to be encountered of the use of _ia_ to refer to inanimates (usually abstract), but this is a feature of the language of some speakers only, and is probably influenced by a knowledge of foreign languages. It is not universally well received. Even in the cases where it is used, it is sporadic; in one and the same writer's works this use of _ia_ or _dia_ may be much more frequent in one section than in another. No tendency towards increase or decrease in use has been noted.

Ia harus memberi kemungkinan untuk setiap waktu menghadapi revisi.
'It (international agreement) must allow for the possibility of effecting revisions at any time.'

Ia bukan pakta antara beberapa negara.
'It (the Conscience of Man) is not a treaty among a certain number of countries.'

Tidakkah modal-modal ini menggembirakan? Tidakkah ia tjukup besar...?
'Are not these capital funds gratifying? Is it not large enough?'

3.1.1.6 The pronoun <u>kita</u> is inclusive in that the speaker includes the hearer when he chooses this pronoun.

kita 'we, including you to whom I am talking'

The pronoun <u>kami</u> is exclusive, on the other hand, in that the speaker excludes the hearer when he uses it.

kami 'we others, excluding you to whom I am talking'

(Very occasionally, <u>kita</u> is used in place of <u>saja</u>, etc., to refer to the speaker alone; this is more colloquial than formal, however, and is especially to be found in the speech of Djakarta.)

3.1.1.7 The symbol <u>N</u> in the table of pronouns represents a noun. It is customary, in addressing a person formally in Indonesian, to use not a pronoun, but a noun. This noun may be the name of the person, if that is known, or his rank, or his relationship to the speaker. A foreigner is customarily addressed as <u>Tuan</u> 'lord, master' if a man, <u>Njonja</u>, 'lady, mistress' if a married woman, <u>Nona</u>, 'lady, miss' if an unmarried woman, and, at least formerly, <u>Noni</u> if a female child. These titles are also occasionally used for Indonesians especially on formal occasions. Much more usual for Indonesians among themselves, in cases where the name or rank is unknown, or even where the name and rank are known but the situation is quite formal, is saudara for either men or women, and saudari specifically for women.

An Indonesian may also, in talking to another Indonesian, confer upon the person to whom he is speaking some honorary family relationship, addressing an older man as father or uncle, a slightly older man as older brother, a slightly younger man as younger brother, and a much younger man as son. Corresponding forms would be used in addressing women. Except for the use of bapak or pak for father and ibu or bu for mother, most of these forms of address are considered less than sophisticated, and tend to be used only on the informal level.

Nouns which are, in effect, titles are also used in conjunction with names, the title occurring before the name.

Tuan Smith	'Mr. Smith'
Saudara Sutjipto	'Mr. Sutjipto'
Ibu Kartini	'Mrs. Kartini'

Frequently, however, a title denoting a family relationship, usually in a reduced form, is joined to a full or reduced form of the person's name, and this produces an effect of respectful intimacy. (Reduced forms of names are produced by the dropping of a number of syllables, usually from the beginning of the name - Section 1.9.)

Bung Karno	'President Sukarno'
Pak Nardjo	'Mr. Sunardjo'
Bu Koesmiati	'Miss (or Mrs.) Koesmiati'

Married couples frequently address each other, at least in literature, as if they were brother and sister. The husband customarily addresses his wife as if she were his younger sister (adik), and the wife addresses her husband as if he were her older brother (kakak).

3.1.1.8 Certain of the pronominal forms, those listed in parentheses in the table, deserve special comment.

Hamba, meaning 'slave', and beta are occasionally found as an equivalent for I in situations where a king or someone in authority is being addressed, but they are by no means common in contemporary Indonesian. It may be noted that the more usual form saja is also said to be derived from a word meaning 'slave'.

Anda is a form derived from the honorific suffix -anda or -nda (see Section 2.2.2). It is used occasionally as a means of addressing a person whose name or title is not yet known. It has also been used in advertisements, where the person or persons being appealed to are very general. It is a neologism which does not seem to be taking firm root.

In an attempt to evolve a form which could be used in addressing people whose names or titles were not known, forms have been borrowed from other languages, including ju from the English you. These forms do not seem to be taking root, either.

3.1.1.9 See also Sections 3.1.2.4 ff. and 3.1.9.

3.1.2 Nouns

The Indonesian noun, like the English noun, is difficult to define structurally in a relatively simple way.

Morphologically, many nouns consist simply of roots, such as *buku* 'book', *orang* 'person', *kuda* 'horse', or *air* 'water'.

Other nouns are morphologically complex. Forms which have the prefixes *per-* or *peN-* without a suffix, forms which have either of these prefixes plus the suffix *-an*, most forms which have the prefix *ke-* and the suffix *-an*, and most forms which have the suffix *-an* without a prefix are all nouns. These forms are described in the chapter on morphology.

Such forms are nouns, then, and forms which function in the same ways are also nouns.

The general characteristics of nouns will now be described.

3.1.2.1 Personal and Non-personal Nouns

Indonesian nouns are divided into two classes, personal and non-personal. The class of personal nouns can be defined semantically as including any noun which refers to a human being; it can be defined syntactically as any noun which, when modified by a number, may occur with the counter noun *orang*.

Personal nouns may be replaced by the pronouns *ia* and *dia* if they are singular, and by the pronoun *mereka* if they are plural. Non-personal nouns are not replaced by a pronoun, but are omitted without replacement if the context is clear, or are repeated in full.

Personal names belong to the class of personal nouns.

There are a number of naming systems used in different parts of Indonesia; these reflect either differing local practices (Javanese, Balinese) or differing foreign influences (Arabic, Dutch, and, to a lesser extent, Chinese).

Local practice tends to the use of single given names, no family name being used. Even when more than one name is given, none of the names is a family name; it may be possible to establish, however, from components of the name, that its bearer moves in a particular level of society, or is related to a particular group of people.

Foreign influences tend to the assignment of a given name or names preceding one name which is traditional in the family, and which serves, in practice, if not always in theory, as a family name or surname.

The custom that wives take their husband's name on marriage is not generally established; it is found to a considerable extent, however, in the classes which have been most exposed to foreign influences. In such cases, the wife uses the title _Njonja_ preceding her husband's name.

(A full discussion of Indonesian names and appropriate modes of address, although a most important part of the language, is complicated and would require much more space than can be devoted to it here.)

In earlier stages of the language, it was quite common to mark personal nouns by preposing the proclitic _si_.

(In the orthography _si_ is sometimes written as one word with the following item if that item does not begin with a capital letter. It is much more common, however, to write it as a separate word.)

This proclitic was regularly used before personal names. It was also used before other parts of speech than nouns to indicate that that part of speech was being used as a name or as a nickname. In the course of time, probably because of its use in forming somewhat ironic or slighting nicknames, such as _si Gemuk_, 'Fatso' for either scrawny or fat persons, it has come to have a connotation of opprobrium, or, at best, of amused tolerance. At the present time older people will still refer to younger members of their family as, for example, _si Ali_, but the younger members of the society dislike this, and avoid it.

Perhaps also the growing tendency, in some families, to keep pet animals and to give them names in which _si_ is used to show that the form is being used as a name is helping to contribute to the decline in the usage of _si_ for human beings.

putih	'white'
si Putih	'Whitey' (a cat)

An exception to the statement that _si_ is a proclitic for personal nouns is the folk tale, where the animal characters such as _kantjil_ 'mouse-deer' are often personified by the prefixing of this proclitic. Thus _si Kantjil_ is a literary personality similar to Brer Rabbit in the Uncle Remus stories.

But there are some cases where the proclitic _si_ continues in active use. One such case is that in which the same form may be both a personal noun and a non-personal noun. For example, nouns formed with the prefixes _per-_ and _peN-_ added to a verb base refer either to the person who performs the action or to the instrument with which it is performed. In such cases, the personal noun may have _si_ preposed to it, while the non-personal noun does not. From the verb _menggali_ 'dig', the derived noun _penggali_ may mean 'digger' or 'shovel'. In cases of possible ambiguity, the form 'digger' may still occur as _si penggali_ (sometimes alternatively _sipenggali_).

Another similar case is that in which an adjective is nominalized by si to form a personal noun, such as si sakit 'the sick man', from sakit 'sick'; the use of si in this way is not declining; it cannot be regarded as increasing either, since new combinations of this type are not easily produced.

A similar proclitic is sang. It seems to have been originally used before names of gods. It is now occasionally used with both personal and non-personal nouns referring to a person or an object which is held in particular honor.

sang ibu	'Mother, motherhood'
sang merah-putih	'the Indonesian flag'

It is also employed in folk tales, usually in connection with the names of the larger and fiercer animals; the tiger, for example, may be addressed or referred to as sang Harimau.

Again, sang, like si, may develop overtones of amusement and mock respect.

Sang klerk...kawin.
'The worthy clerk...gets married.'

Occasionally, of late, the proclitic sang has also been used in a derogatory fashion, and ironically. Thus, in the political unrest in 1966, President Soekarno was rather sneeringly referred to as Sang Presiden. It remains to be seen whether this proclitic will acquire a pejorative connotation before it becomes obsolete.

Other proclitics of a similar nature (hang, dang) are quite obsolete in contemporary Indonesian.

3.1.2.2 Countable and Uncountable Nouns

Indonesian nouns can be divided into countable and uncountable nouns.

Countable nouns are those which, in contemporary Indonesian, can be directly modified by a numerative without the occurrence of a counter noun between the numerative and the countable noun: anak 'child' (dua anak 'two children'), medja 'table' (dua medja 'two tables'). Uncountable nouns are those which cannot be directly modified by a numerative: air 'water' (dua liter air 'two liters of water'), beras 'rice' (dua kilo beras 'two kilos of rice').

Personal nouns which are proper names of individuals are not used in conjunction with numeratives. All other personal nouns are countable. Non-personal nouns may be countable or uncountable.

3.1.2.3 Plural Formations

A characteristic of countable nouns is that they may freely enter formations which are specifically plural. Uncountable nouns rarely, if ever, do so.

The plural of personal nouns can be specified by the use of kaum or para before the noun. Para is a proclitic which must precede a noun and which refers to a group or collection of people. Kaum is itself a noun, and refers to an ethnic or social group; it is not necessarily used, however, only with names of ethnic and social groups.

Badui	'Bedouin, nomad'
kaum Badui	'the Bedouins'
tani	'farmer'
kaum tani	'agricultural people, peasants'
kaum intelektuil	'intelligentsia'
pembatja	'reader'
para pembatja	'readers'

pegawai	'office worker'
para pegawai	'office workers'

Occasionally, nouns which are made plural with para and kaum are also reduplicated.

para pegawai-pegawai	'office workers'

Any countable noun can be reduplicated to form the plural (see Section 2.1.1.5), whether it is personal or non-personal.

buku	'book'
buku-buku	'books, different kinds of books'
orang	'person'
orang-orang	'people, different kinds of persons'
kuda	'horses'
kuda-kuda	'horses, different kinds of horses'

(It should be recalled that the reduplication of a noun produces, in some cases, another singular noun.)

kuda	'horse'
kuda-kuda	'trestle, sawhorse'
mata	'eye'
mata-mata	'spy'

Nouns which are formed by reduplication in this way are not usually reduplicated again to form the plural.

(In the same way, compound nouns such as tanah air 'native country', are not commonly reduplicated to form the plural; in most cases the meaning is such that a plural formation would be unlikely to occur.)

The uncountable noun, if reduplicated, can have only the connotation of variety.

minjak-minjak	'different kinds of oil'
kaju-kaju	'different kinds of wood'

3.1.2.4 When nouns and pronouns are made negative, the adjunct <u>bukan</u> 'not' occurs before them.

bukan saja	'not I'
bukan dokter	'not a doctor'

3.1.2.5 The interrogative form for pronouns and personal nouns is <u>siapa</u> 'who?' while that for impersonal nouns is <u>apa</u> 'what?'.

Ini apa?	'What is this?'
Ini siapa?	'Who is this?'
Namanja siapa?	'What is his name?'

3.1.2.6 The indefinite form for non-personal nouns is

apa-apa	'anything'
apa sadja	'anything you please'

The indefinite form for personal nouns and pronouns is

siapa sadja	'anyone you please'
barang siapa	'anyone at all'

3.1.3 Numeratives

Numeratives are divided into two classes, those which do not occur with counter nouns, and those which may do so. Numeratives which occur with counter nouns are again divided into two classes, numbers and non-numbers.

3.1.3.1 The one numerative which does not occur with counter nouns is:

tiap-tiap	'each, every'

3.1.3.2 The numeratives which may occur with counter nouns and which are not themselves numbers are:

segala	'all'
banjak	'many'
semua	'all'
masing-masing	'each'
seluruh	'all'

Of these segala and banjak, when they occur without counter nouns, may occur with reduplicated countable nouns; the others do not occur with reduplicated nouns.

3.1.3.3 The remaining numeratives are the numbers, and these are:

satu, suatu, se-	'one'
dua	'two'
tiga	'three'
empat	'four'
lima	'five'
enam	'six'
tudjuh	'seven'
delapan	'eight'
sembilan	'nine'
sepuluh	'ten'
sebelas, seblas	'eleven'
duabelas	'twelve'
tigabelas	'thirteen'
delapanbelas	'eighteen'
sembilanbelas	'nineteen'
duapuluh	'twenty'
duapuluh satu, duapuluh dua, etc.	'twenty-one, twenty-two, etc.'
tigapuluh	'thirty'
delapanpuluh	'eighty'

sembilanpuluh	'ninety'
seratus	'one hundred'
dua ratus	'two hundred'
tiga ratus	'three hundred'
delapan ratus	'eight hundred'
sembilan ratus	'nine hundred'
seribu	'one thousand'
dua ribu	'two thousand'
sedjuta	'one million'
tiga djuta	'three million'

Complex numbers are formed on the principle that a smaller number before a larger multiplies that larger number, while a smaller number after a larger number is added to that larger number. The numbers from 11 through 19 form a subsystem of their own.

duapuluh satu	'twenty-one'
empat ratus limapuluh enam	'four hundred fifty-six'
seribu sembilan ratus empatpuluh lima	'one thousand nine hundred forty-five (1945)'

Nouns used with a numeral are not reduplicated. There is the occasional exceptional case.

Apakah maksud lima kata-kata berturut-turut ini...?
'What is the point of these five expressions linked together like this...?'

The number 'one' is ordinarily <u>satu</u>. The proclitic <u>se</u>- is ordinarily used with counter nouns and as a prefix to other numbers; it is closely akin to the prefix <u>se</u>- which is described in the chapter on Morphology, Section 2.9). The form <u>suatu</u> is also used for <u>satu</u>; there is a tendency for it to be used in much the same way as the English indefinite article 'a' or 'an'.

satu pendapat	'one opinion'
suatu pendapat	'an opinion'

The suffix -belas, used to form the numbers from 11 through 19, is also written -blas.

3.1.3.4 A set of collective numerals is formed by prefixing ke- to the numbers given here.

kedua	'a set of two'
ketiga	'a set of three'

(These belong in the class of numeratives and are not to be confused with the ordinal numerals, which belong in the form-class of adjectives.

pertama	'first'
kedua	'second'
ketiga	'third'
kedua orang	'the two men'
orang kedua	'the second man')

Another set of collective numerals is formed by prefixing ber- to the numbers. These may function as numeratives or as predicatives.

Beribu-ribu maaf!	'A thousand pardons!'

3.1.3.5 Numeratives are not customarily made negative; sentences in which a numerative would be made negative are recast so as to avoid such a contingency.

3.1.3.6 The interrogative form for numeratives is berapa 'how much?', 'how many?'

3.1.3.7 The indefinite form for numeratives is beberapa 'a certain number', berapa sadja 'as many as you please'.

3.1.4 Counter Nouns

The counter nouns form a diminishing, and perhaps disappearing, class of words in Indonesian. Formerly, numbers could be used only with members of a specific set of counter nouns, which interposed between the number and the noun referring to the object being counted. These counter nouns were, and continue to be, nouns with a specific meaning in their own right. Thus, the noun _ekor_ 'tail', was the counter noun for animals, birds and fishes. In counting horses, it was necessary to interpose _ekor_ between the numeral and the noun for horse, _kuda_.

seekor kuda	'one horse'
dua ekor kuda	'two horses'
sepuluh ekor kuda	'ten horses'

The following list gives some examples of counter nouns, but no attempt has been made to make the list exhaustive.

Counter	Meaning	For counting
orang	'human being'	human beings
ekor	'tail'	animals, birds, fish, etc.
buah	'fruit'	objects in general, and particularly roundish objects
bidji	'seed'	small objects
batang	'stick'	long, cylindrical objects
helai	'sheet'	paper, cloth, etc.
gugus	'cluster'	clusters of objects
keping	'chip'	slices, flat objects, leaves
miang	'grain, drop'	grains of sand, drops of water
patah	'piece'	words
putjuk	'sprout'	guns, letters
sikat	'brush'	bunches of bananas
tepek	'slab, cake'	fat, loaf sugar, etc.
tjarik	'strip'	paper, cloth
utas	'piece of string'	string, cord
tjatuk	'spoonful'	liquid
tjekak	'pinch'	salt, pepper, etc.

litar	'litre'
metar	'metre'
kilo	'kilogram'

In contemporary Indonesian, the number of counter nouns in common use has been considerably reduced. Those which are now most common are:

orang	'human being'	for human beings
ekor	'tail'	for animals
buah	'fruit'	for anything else

The use of even these counter nouns has been further reduced. Most speakers avoid them on ordinary occasions, except after the number _one_, which frequently occurs in its proclitic alternant _se-_. Thus, 'one student' will probably occur as _seorang mahasiswa_, but 'two students' is much more likely to occur as _dua mahasiswa_ rather than _dua orang mahasiswa_.

With counter nouns:

Untuk memberikan sepatah dua patah kata pengantar.
'In order to give one or two words of introduction.'

Without counter nouns:

Apakah maksud lima kata-kata berturut-turut ini?
'What is the purpose of these five expressions linked together like this?'

Dangan satu medja, empat kursi, satu zitje, satu tempat tidur...
'With one table, four chairs, one settee, one bed...'

3.1.5 Determiners

The determiners are _ini_ 'this' and _itu_ 'that'.

Itu also occurs extensively as the marker of the end of a nominal expansion. In such a case, its meaning of 'that' may be negligible or non-existent.

Itu also occurs with a nominalizing function, to indicate that a structure which is not ordinarily a nominal structure has the value of a nominal structure. See Section 3.1.6.2.

3.1.6 Nominalizations

Individual words or syntactic arrangements of words, if they are not nominals, may be converted to nominals by one of the following nominalization processes.

3.1.6.1 The prefixing of the adjunct jang to any predicative (a verb or an adjective) produces a nominalization of that predicative.

pergi	'go'
jang pergi	'(the one) who goes'
membelikan saja buku itu kemarin	'bought me that book yesterday'
jang membelikan saja buku itu kemarin	'(the one) who bought me that book yesterday'
biru	'blue'
jang biru	'(the one) which is blue'
sudah kaja	'already rich'
jang sudah kaja	'(the one) who is already rich'
lebih besar	'bigger'
jang lebih besar	'(the one) which is bigger'
dikamar lain	'in the other room'
jang dikamar lain	'(the one) which is in the other room'

The adjunct jang may be used also with the determiners ini and itu. This usage is fairly uncommon because, since the determiners are nominals, the addition of the particle jang has no effect except to render them more emphatic, especially in situations of contrast.

Ada dua buku diatas medja. Jang ini buku sedjarah. Jang itu buku ilmu bumi.
'There are two books on the table. This one is a history book, while that one is a geography book.'

3.1.6.2 Predicative forms (i.e. verbs and adjectives) are occasionally converted into nominals simply by using the predicative form in a syntactic position characteristically occupied by a nominal.

(The predicatives being used as nominals in the following examples are underlined.)

Hak menguasai dari Negara.
'The State's right to sovereignty'

berdjalan kaki dengan tiada bersepatu
'walk barefoot (without wearing shoes)'

Tetapi memburu mangsa untuk dimakannja sendiri tidaklah lagi dilakukannja.
'But killing prey for its own eating is no longer in its pattern of behavior.'

This procedure may, on occasion, give rise to ambiguity. The ambiguity can be obviated either by adding itu to the end of the construction being used as a noun, or by adding the enclitic -nja to the form which is being used as a noun. In such cases, neither itu nor the enclitic -nja has a specific meaning, but simply serves to mark the form or construct as a nominalization.

kemungkinan akan tertjapainja funksi bumi
'the possibility of realizing the function of the land'

Hidup dengan dua betina atau lebih itu dinamai polygami.
'Living with two or more females is called polygamy.'

Both itu and -nja can therefore be classed in such cases as nominal markers. Their occurrence is not limited to nominalizing adjectives and verbs, however. Used with nouns, they tend to make the noun definite, and so are coming to fulfil a function very much like that of the definite article 'the' in English.

orang	'a person'
orang itu	'the person'

These markers are to be differentiated from the determiner itu 'that' and the enclitic pronoun -nja 'his, her, their'.

3.1.6.3 It has been pointed out above that the proclitic si (and sang, etc.) can occur with adjectives and other forms in order to make proper names of them; since such proper names are nominals, this is another nominalization process.

3.1.6.4 Nominalizations, like nouns, are made negative when necessary by preposing bukan.

bukan jang biru	'not the blue one'

But, if a negative construct is nominalized, the negative is retained in the same form. (Usually tidak occurs.)

Untuk tidak merugikan kepentingan umum...
'In order not to impair the common good...'

3.1.6.5 The interrogative form of the _jang_-nominalization is _jang mana_ 'which?'. This is also the interrogative form for adjectives which modify nouns.

buku jang mana? 'which book?'

Occasionally _mana_ occurs without _jang_ in this construct, but this is rather informal; sometimes it is used for stylistic purposes to avoid the repetition of _jang_.

buku mana? 'which book?'
Belum tentu mana jang lebih gelukkig.
'It is not yet certain which is the luckier.'

3.1.7 Nominal Expansions

Any simple noun can be expanded into an endocentric construct with the noun as its head by the addition of other nominals, and of adjectives. When such an expansion occurs, the components are in fixed positional relationship to the head-noun and to each other.

The head-noun will be underlined in the examples which are given in the following discussion.

3.1.7.1 A head-noun may be preceded by the verb root _punja_ 'have', preceded in turn by a pronoun.

Saja punja _rumah_.
'My house' (spoken with sentence intonation, this could mean instead 'I have a house').

This particular construction is completely anomalous in Indonesian structure. It has the same meaning as the structure

rumah saja 'my house'

and so there is no absolute requirement that it be used. Many speakers avoid it. Nonetheless, many other speakers continue to use it. Sometimes, in the orthography, pronoun and verb are written as one word.

Kalau saudara-saudara membuka saja punja dada,
dan melihat saja punja hati,
'If you open my chest and look at my heart,'

Rakjat tidak tertjukupi minimal iapunja sandang
dan iapunja pangan.
'The people are not endowed with enough to constitute the minimum for their food and for their clothing.'

If the noun is premodified by this construction, then it is not usually premodified by any other forms.

3.1.7.2 The head-noun may be preceded by a numerative.

banjak orang	'many people'
tiga kuda	'three horses'
tiap-tiap hari	'every day'

Since the numeratives specify a particular number, or at least specify singular or plural, it is uncommon for the head-noun to be reduplicated. Occasionally, however, reduplicated forms appear after banjak and segala.

banjak anak	'many children'
banjak anak-anak	
segala pagawai	'all the office-workers'
segala pegawai-pegawai	

3.1.7.3 The head-noun may be preceded by a counter noun, provided that the counter noun is in turn preceded by one of the numeratives which occur with counter nouns.

banjak orang pegawai	'many office-workers'
tiga ekor kuda	'three horses'
sebuah buku	'one book'

3.1.7.4 The head-noun may be followed by another noun which is in apposition to it. It is perhaps debatable in such a case whether the first noun or the second noun is the head of the construction, and it is perhaps easiest to regard nouns in apposition as a unit, and equally head of their construction.

Presiden Sukarno	'President Sukarno'
Tuan Smith	'Mr. Smith'
Djeneral Sudirman	'General Sudirman'

The head-noun may also be followed by another noun which modifies it. The second noun refers to the specific application to which the reference of the head noun is delimited.

rumah doktor	'the doctor's house'
anak Mala	'Mala's child'
ekor kuda	'the horse's tail'
orang Djawa	'Javanese person'
mangkok kopi	'coffee cup'
buku sedjarah	'history book'
ilmu bumi	'geography (earth science)'
kain batik	'batik cloth'

The noun which follows the head-noun, and modifies it or is in apposition to it, is itself capable of being expanded according to the patterns described here. Theoretically, any degree of expansion is possible; practically, no premodifiers ordinarily occur, and no complex postmodification is found, since such a combination would be regarded as clumsy, and therefore stylistically bad.

On occasion the relationship of the head-noun and the modifying noun may be marked by the preposition dari before the modifying noun, particularly where the meaning of the modification structure refers to possession of the referent of the head, or to participation in the referent of the head. This usage is deprecated by some grammarians, but it seems to be growing; if the noun structures are complicated, the occurrence of the preposition is a definite aid to clarity.

sebagai "Kaitjoo" (ketua) dari "Dokuritsu Zyunbi Tyoosakai"
'as "Kaitjoo" (chairman) of the "Dokuritsu Zyunbi Tyoosakai"'

Hak menguasai dari Negara
'The State's right to sovereignty'

kesatuan tanah-air dari seluruh rakjat Indonesia
'a union of the native lands of all the peoples of Indonesia'

The numbers may also occur in this position after the head; they then indicate that the head-noun bears that particular number as a distinguishing mark.

<u>halaman</u> dua puluh	'page twenty'
<u>kamar</u> tiga	'room three'
<u>djam</u> empat	'four o'clock'
<u>tanggal</u> tudjuhbelas Agustus	'the seventeenth of August'

Noun modifiers are not customarily made negative.

Noun modifiers are made interrogative in the same way as nouns, by the use of <u>apa</u> 'what?' or <u>siapa</u> 'who?'.

<u>buku</u> apa?	'what kind of book?'
<u>buku</u> sedjarah	'a history book'
<u>buku</u> siapa?	'whose book?'
<u>buku</u> saja	'my book'

3.1.7.5 The head-noun may be followed by an adjective which modifies it.

buku besar	'the big book'
kain biru	'the blue cloth'
kuda kuat	'the strong horse'

If the head-noun is postmodified by a noun, the adjective will follow the modifying noun. This situation, however, creates an ambiguity under certain circumstances because it may not be clear whether the adjective modifies the head-noun or the modifying noun. Thus, in buku sedjarah lama, it is unclear whether this is 'an old history book', or 'a book of ancient history'. It has been stated that in such a case lama must be taken to modify sedjarah, to which it stands nearest, and that the meaning is consequently 'a book of ancient history'; it would be necessary, according to this contention, to nominalize the adjective (jang lama) in order to make it quite clear that lama is to be construed with buku; thus, 'an old history book' would necessarily be rendered as buku sedjarah jang lama. This statement, however, seems to be more of a prescription as to how certain grammarians feel that speakers of Bahasa Indonesia ought to speak rather than a description of how they actually do. Many Indonesians do not subscribe to the rule as stated here, but are content to consider the structure completely ambiguous.

Adjectives which are themselves modified do not usually modify a noun directly. Instead, the modified adjective is nominalized by the preposing of jang, and this nominalization modifies the noun in the manner usual for nominalizations.

orang kaja	'the rich man'
orang jang baru kaja	'the newly-rich man'

3.1.7.6 The head-noun may be followed by a pronoun which modifies it. This is the modification of possession.

buku saja	'my book'
kudanja	'his, her horse'

If the noun is also postmodified by another noun, or by an adjective, the pronoun will follow this noun or this adjective.

buku sedjarah saja	'my history book'
buku ilmu bumi saja	'my geography book'
buku biru saja	'my blue book'

If, however, the noun is modified by a noun and by an adjective and by a pronoun, all three, then the adjective must be nominalized by preposing the particle jang, and the nominalization will then follow the pronoun, as nominalizations customarily do.

buku sedjarah saja jang biru	'my blue history book'

3.1.7.7 The head-noun may be followed by a nominalization which modifies it. Such a nominalization will occur after any modifying noun, adjective or pronoun.

doktor jang tinggal di Djalan Sabang
'the doctor who lives on Sabang Street'

doktor gigi saja jang tinggal di Djalan Sabang
'my dentist who lives on Sabang Street'

buku biru jang besar
'the large blue book'

Prepositional constructs usually modify nouns only when nominalized by jang.

buku-buku jang diatas medja
'the books on the table'

Occasionally, however, prepositional constructs may modify the noun directly; they are usually the only post-modifier, except nouns, to occur.

mahasiswa di Djakarta
'the students in Djakarta

hukum adat tentang tanah
'the common law as regards land'

3.1.7.8 The head-noun may be followed by a determiner which modifies it. The determiner is always the last of all noun modifiers, and so it serves to mark the end of the noun expansion.

<u>buku</u> itu	'that book'
<u>buku</u> sedjarah itu	'that history book'
<u>buku</u> sedjarah saja jang biru itu	'that blue history book of mine'

3.1.7.9 The possibilities of the noun expansion may be schematized as follows; zero represents the position of the noun-head, the negative numbers the positions preceding the head, and the positive numbers the positions following the head.

-2 Pronoun - <u>punja</u>, providing no numerative occurs
-2 Numeratives
-1 Count nouns, provided that there is a numerative and that the numerative is one which occurs with count nouns
0 The Noun-Head and Nouns in Apposition
+1 Noun Modifiers
+2 Adjective Modifiers, provided that the adjective modifier is itself unmodified and that there is not both a noun modifier (+1) and a pronoun modifier (+3); in these cases the adjective must be nominalized by means of the proclitic <u>jang</u>, and assumes position +4.
+3 Pronoun Modifier

+4 Nominalizations with _jang_, prepositional constructs
+5 Determiner

3.1.8 Partial Nominal Constructs

The noun-head expansion continues to function as a nominal construct under circumstances where the noun-head itself is not present. These partial expansions may consist of the following combinations of modifiers:

a) a numerative

banjak 'a lot'

b) a numerative plus a count noun

tiga ekor 'three head'

c) a nominalization introduced by the particle _jang_

jang biru 'the blue one'

d) a determiner

itu 'that one'

Naturally, such partial nominal constructs occur only in response situations where it is clear from the preceding sentences or from the circumstances which noun-head is intended.

3.1.9 Pronoun-head Constructs

Pronouns can be expanded only to a limited extent. They are not premodified by numerals or count nouns. They may occur in apposition with nouns which themselves may be expanded. They are not postmodified by adjectives or by other pronouns. They may, however, be postmodified by nominalizations introduced by the particle _jang_; again, the effect is ordinarily that of apposition. It sometimes happens that they are postmodified by determiners; the combination mereka itu 'those people there' or 'those people who have been mentioned' is relatively common.

kami, mahasiswa-mahasiswa Universitas Indonesia
'we, the students of the University of Indonesia'

kamu jang pandai
'you, who are clever'

Kita ini berani merdéka, atau tidak?
'Do we here dare to be free, or not?'

Mereka jang 92 djuta banjaknja
'They who are 92 millions in number'

3.2 Predicatives

The name 'Predicative' has been assigned to this form-class because its members serve as predicates in sentence structures (Section 4.2 ff.), although they are not the only type of predicate which can be found. Predicatives include almost all morphologically complex forms which have not been described as nominals; in particular, those formed with the prefixes ber-, meN-, and ter- are predicatives. Most forms with the prefix se-, and those forms with ke- -an which are described as verbs also belong to the class of predicatives. Morphologically simple forms which have the same pattern of distribution as these are also predicatives.

3.2.1 Verbs and Adjectives

While all predicates have certain features of structure in common, they exhibit a number of differences which make it advisable to subdivide them into two classes: verbs and adjectives.

Verbs and adjectives differ from each other morphologically to some extent, but most particularly in the way in which they combine syntactically with other form-classes.

3.2.1.1 Most adjectives are morphologically simple, that is, they consist of roots without affixes.

besar	'big'
senang	'happy'
tua	'old'

There are, of course, adjectives which are morphologically complex, occurring with the prefixes ber- and ter-, or with ke- prefixed to numeratives.

bersedjarah	'historical'
tertutup	'closed'
ketiga	'third'

Most verbs, on the other hand, are morphologically complex; all forms which occur with the prefix meN-, many forms which occur with the prefixes ber- and ter-, and a few which occur with the complex ke- -an are verbs.

mendarat	'go ashore'
mendaratkan	'set (O) ashore'
beristeri	'be married'
tertawa	'laugh'
kehudjanan	'be caught in the rain'

There are also verbs which are morphologically simple. Indeed, some of the commonest verbs in the language are of this type. These include many verbs referring to movement or to lack of movement, and a number referring to everyday activities; almost all are intransitive (Section 3.2.3).

pergi	'go'
datang	'come'
kembali	'return'
pulang	'return home'

masuk	'enter'
lalu	'pass'
lari	'run'
tinggal	'stay'
turun	'descend'
naik	'ascend'
pindah	'change place'
diam	'stay'
tiba	'arrive'
sampai	'arrive'
mandi	'bathe'

Those simple verbs which are transitive have also a morphologically complex counterpart; the passive forms are derived from these.

makan	'eat'
memakan	
dimakan	'be eaten'
minum	'drink'
meminum	
diminum	'be drunk'
tahu	'know'
mengetahui	
diketahui	'be known'

The auxiliary verbs (Section 3.2.2) are also morphologically simple.

Many verbs which are morphologically complex in formal Indonesian become morphologically simple in colloquial speech, and the tendency to use such forms is increasing even on more formal levels. For this reason, no list of verbs which are commonly used without affixes can be complete, because the list is not stable.

3.2.1.2 Adjectives differ from verbs syntactically in that they postmodify nouns either directly, or when nominalized by the preposing of <u>jang</u>. Verbs never postmodify nouns directly, but only when nominalized with <u>jang</u>.

3.2.1.3 Adjectives also enter into the structures described in Section 3.2.4 as the comparison of adjectives. Verbs do not, ordinarily.

3.2.1.4 With these comparatively minor differences, however, adjectives and verbs (i.e. predicatives) function in the same way.

3.2.2 Auxiliaries

All predicatives can be modified by certain morphologically simple predicatives which function in the language structure as a special kind of verb. These specialized predicatives are here called auxiliaries. The auxiliaries are developing a tendency toward a fixed order when they occur together, and they can be described as occupying a series of three positions before the predicative which serves as the head. It is this tendency toward a fixed order which differentiates them from other premodifiers of predicatives.

3.2.2.1 The first class of auxiliaries contains _akan_, which denotes futurity.

Ali akan pergi. 'Ali will go.'

3.2.2.2 The second class of auxiliaries contains _harus_; it denotes an inescapable obligation, and is equivalent to the English 'must'.

Ali akan harus pergi. 'Ali will have to go.'

(The forms _mesti_, _pasti_, _perlu_ and _(tidak) usah_, which have more or less the same meaning, and which can occur in the same relative position in the predicate, can also occur in other positions, and, on the whole, are more akin to the other premodifiers than to the auxiliaries.)

3.2.2.3 The third class of auxiliaries can be divided into two subclasses. One subclass contains _sanggup_ 'to be willing to', _boleh_ 'to be permitted to', _bisa_ or _dapat_ 'to be able to', and _hendak_ 'to want to'. The auxiliaries of this subclass are followed only by predicatives.

The other subclass includes ingin 'wish', suka 'like' and mau 'want'. The auxiliaries of this second subclass are followed either by predicatives or by nominals.

Ali mau kopi.	'Ali wants coffee.'
Ali mau pergi.	'Ali wants to go.'
Ali bisa pergi.	'Ali can go.'
Ali mau tinggi.	'Ali wants to be tall.'
Ali akan harus mau bekerdja.	'Ali will have to want to work.'

3.2.2.4 Any predicative may be preceded by one or more of these auxiliaries under the usual conditions for order classes, namely, that there may be either one member of any class or none in any predicate construct, and that those auxiliaries which do occur will occur in the specified order.

The order for auxiliaries is therefore:

-3	akan
-2	harus
-1	boleh, bisa, dapat, hendak, sanggup; ingin, mau, suka
0	the predicative head

3.2.3 Dependencies of Verbs

Any predicative may function as the head of a predicate construct. It can be preceded by auxiliaries (Section 3.2.2); it can be modified by the predicative modifiers (Section 3.3.1). In addition, any particular predicative may require, or may frequently occur with, other following constructs which it governs, and which will be referred to here as dependencies. Verbs occur more frequently with dependencies than adjectives, and the patterns of verb dependencies are quite different from those of adjectives. It will therefore be useful to describe verb dependencies separately.

3.2.3.1 One type of verb requires no dependency; it is intransitive.

Ia mandi.	'He is bathing.'
Ia beristeri.	'He is married.'
Ia menari.	'He is dancing.'
Ia tertawa.	'He laughs.'
Ia kehudjanan.	'He gets caught in the rain.'

3.2.3.2 A second type of verb may have a verb as a dependency; this is particularly the case with verbs which refer to movement; as has been pointed out, most such verbs are morphologically simple; they are intransitive, since their verbal dependency does not constitute an object, and there is no corresponding passive construction.

Mala pergi.
'Mala has gone.'

Mala pergi membeli beras.
'Mala has gone to buy rice.'

Ibu datang.
'The old woman has come.'

Ibu datang memindjam uang.
'The old woman has come to borrow money.'

3.2.3.3 A third type of verb occurs with either a nominal construct or an adjective as a dependency. These verbs are here referred to as copulative, and their dependency, whether adjective or nominal, is referred to as a complement. Such verbs constitute another type of intransitive verb, since the complement does not constitute an object, and no corresponding passive construct exists.

Adiknja mendjadi tinggi sekali.
'His little brother grew very tall.'

Adiknja mendjadi tentara.
'His little brother became a soldier.'

3.2.3.4 A fourth type of verb is one that occurs on occasion without a dependency, in which case it is intransitive, and on occasion with a nominal construct as its single object, in which case it is transitive. Verbs of this sort, which function in either way, may be called amphoteric. When they are morphologically complex, they have forms typical of transitive verbs. When they have an object, the corresponding passive construct exists.

Ia membatja.
'He is reading.'

Ia membatja buku itu.
'He is reading the book.'

Siti lagi makan.
'Siti is still eating.'

Siti makan pisang.
'Siti is eating a banana.'

3.2.3.5 A fifth type of verb occurs with a single object which is a nominal construct; such verbs are transitive. Many verbs which have the prefix meN- are transitive. All verbs which have the prefix meN- and either the suffix -kan or the suffix -i are transitive if not doubly transitive. The corresponding passive construct exists.

Ali membawa beras.
'Ali is bringing the rice.'

Saja akan membeli buku itu.
'I am going to buy that book.'

Petani itu mengairi sawahnja.
'The farmer irrigates his rice field.'

Amat sudah mendinginkan bir.
'Amat has already iced the beer.'

3.2.3.6 A sixth type of verb occurs with two objects, each of which is a nominal construct;

such verbs are doubly transitive. If a verb compounded of the prefix meN- and a base is transitive, then the verb compounded of the prefix meN-, the same base, and either the suffix -kan or -i is frequently doubly transitive. The corresponding passive construct exists, but there are restrictions as to which object of the active will occur as the subject of the passive.

Ali membawa beras. (transitive)
'Ali is bringing the rice.'

Ali membawakan saja beras itu. (doubly transitive)
'Ali is bringing me the rice.'

Saja akan membeli buku itu. (transitive)
'I am going to buy that book.'

Saja akan membelikan Siti buku itu. (doubly transitive)
'I am going to buy that book for Siti.'

Ali mengirim surat. (transitive)
'Ali sent a letter.'

Ali mengirimi adiknja surat. (doubly transitive)
'Ali sent his younger brother a letter.'

3.2.3.7 A seventh type of verb has as its dependency an object and an object complement; the object is a nominal construct, while the complement is a nominal construct or an adjective. Such verbs are here called transitive-copulative verbs. The corresponding passive construct exists, in which the object becomes the subject of the passive construct. (It is this fact which precludes considering this simply as a verb followed by a clause without an introductory conjunction, an interpretation which would otherwise be quite in order.)

Dia menjangka saja orang Palembang.
'He thought I was a Palembang man.'

Dia mengira saja sakit.
'He thought I was sick.'

3.2.3.8 An eighth type of verb has as its dependency a dependent clause consisting of the conjunction <u>bahwa</u> and a sentence structure.

Ia mengatakan bahwa Ali belum selesai.
'He says that Ali is not yet finished.'

In some cases, <u>bahwa</u> does not occur.

Ia mengatakan Ali belum selesai.
'He says that Ali is not yet finished.'

If the subject of the verb in the dependent clause and the subject of the independent verb have the same referent, the subject of the dependent clause may not occur.

Ia mengatakan belum selesai.
'He says that he himself has not yet finished.'

The corresponding passive construct may occur if the conjunction <u>bahwa</u> is retained, but such passives are very rare.

3.2.3.9 A ninth type of verb has a sentence structure as its dependency, but the sentence structure is not introduced by a conjunction. (In certain cases, a conjunction may be introduced without a change of meaning.)

Ali memaksa adiknja minum obat.
(Ali memaksa supaja adiknja minum obat.)
'Ali made his younger brother take the medicine.'

3.2.4 Comparison of Adjectives

Adjectives can serve as the head of expansions which are conventionally described as the comparison of adjectives. Verbs cannot do so, ordinarily.

3.2.4.1 The adjective itself serves as the positive form.

Rumah itu mahal.
'That house is expensive.'

3.2.4.2 The comparative of superiority is formed by preposing lebih.

Rumah ini lebih mahal.
'This house is more expensive.'

A direct comparison between two items utilizes the preposition dari or daripada before the inferior item.

Rumah ini lebih mahal daripada rumah itu.
'This house is more expensive than that house.'

3.2.4.3 The comparative of inferiority is formed by preposing kurang.

Rumah ini kurang mahal.
'This house is less expensive.'

A direct comparison between two items utilizes the preposition dari or daripada after the adjective and before the superior item.

Rumah ini kurang mahal daripada rumah itu.
'This house is less expensive than that house.'

3.2.4.4 The comparative of equality is formed by adding the prefix se- to the adjective, and following it with the preposition dengan.

Rumah ini semahal dengan rumah itu.
'This house is as expensive as that one.'

Occasionally the preposition dengan may not occur.

Rumah ini semahal rumah itu.
'This house is as expensive as that one.'

Another possibility utilizes _sama_ before the adjective and adds the enclitic _-nja_ to it; the preposition _dengan_ occurs, in this construct.

Rumah ini sama mahalnja dengan rumah itu.
'This house is as expensive as that one.'

3.2.4.5 The superlative of comparison is formed by preposing _paling_ to the adjective. The combination is then frequently nominalized by preposing _jang_.

Orang jang paling pandai.
'The cleverest man'

Another superlative is formed by adding the prefix _ter-_ to the adjective.

orang terpandai
'the cleverest man, a most clever man, an exceedingly clever man'

In cases where the adjective is formed by the addition of the prefix _ber-_, only the superlative with _paling_ occurs.

berguna	'useful'
paling berguna	'most useful'

3.2.5 Dependencies of Adjectives

Adjectives do not generally govern dependencies. There are, however, certain exceptions.

3.2.5.1 Some adjectives govern predicatives.

berani
'brave'
Ia berani memegang ular sendok itu.
'He dared to pick up that cobra.'
Kita ini berani merdeka atau tidak?
'Do we here dare to be free, or do we not?'

takut
'afraid'
Saja takut masuk disana.
'I am afraid to go in there.'

pandai
'clever'
Ali pandai berbahasa Inggeris.
'Ali knows how to speak English.'

tjekat
'adept'
Luak lebih tjekat memandjat dari pada kera!
'A civet cat is more adept at climbing than a monkey!'

3.2.5.2 Some adjectives govern prepositional constructions.

takut
'afraid'
Mina takut akan andjing besar itu.
'Mina is afraid of that big dog.'

bangga
'proud'
Ia bangga sekali akan anaknja.
'He is very proud of his child.'

3.2.5.3 Some adjectives govern clause constructions.

jakin
'certain'
Saja jakin bahwa saudara akan berhasil.
'I am certain that you will succeed.'

3.2.5.4 Most adjectives may be followed by a noun to which the suffix -nja is added. The noun delimits the area of application of the adjective.

sama tangkasnja dengan lutung
'equal in agility to a monkey'

binatang jang hitam rupanja
'an animal with a black face'

3.3 Adjuncts

Adjuncts comprise a number of forms which are generally morphologically simple, and which, when complex, show no overall pattern of morphological patterning. They serve a variety of functions in different constructs, but do not serve as the head of a construct (except occasionally, when one adjunct is modified by another).

One group of adjuncts contains forms which modify predicatives and nominals; these are called modifiers (Section 3.3.1).

Another group of adjuncts contains forms which indicate the interrelationships of various constructs; these are called ordinators. Coordinators (Section 3.4) and connectives (Section 3.5) join various kinds of construct on a basis of syntactic equality. Subordinators (Section 3.6) govern constructs of a fixed type, and so form exocentric constructions which serve as modifiers to other constructs.

3.3.1 Modifiers

Modifiers can be classed as predicative modifiers or nominal modifiers, depending on whether they modify predicatives or nominals, but the distinction is not hard and fast. More important is the classification into premodifiers, which occur before the head which they modify, and post-modifiers, which occur after the head which they modify. A few modifiers occur indifferently either before or after their head.

A premodifier may modify the head verb or adjective in a predicate, in which case it may occur either immediately before the head, or, as is more usual when there are auxiliaries, before the first auxiliary.

A premodifier may also modify a particular auxiliary, in which case it occurs immediately before that auxiliary.

Occasionally a premodifier may modify another premodifier.

3.3.1.1 The negative for predicatives is the premodifier tidak. It sometimes occurs in the forms tak, which is somewhat less formal on the whole (but is found on a formal level when it negates an adjective), or tiada, which is somewhat more formal and affective. When the negative modifies the entire predicative structure, it customarily occurs before any other member of the structure, including any other premodifier. When, however, it premodifies a specific item in the predicate, it is preposed to that item. Tidak does not premodify sudah.

Ia tidak harus pergi.
'He does not have to go.'

Ia harus tidak pergi.
'He must not go.'

Burung tak boleh tidak harus giat.
'A bird cannot be made to be inactive.'

Dimana-mana orang merasa tak puas.
'Everywhere people feel discontented.'

Kekuasaan Kepala Negara tidak tak terbatas.
'The power of the Chief of State is not unlimited.'

Tidak may occur without the head which it modifies if the head can be supplied from the context.

Mau merdeka atau tidak?
'Do you want to be free or not?'

Diseblah demokrasi politik harus pula berlaku demokrasi ekonomi. Kalau tidak, manusia belum merdeka.
'Alongside the political democracy, there must also exist an economic democracy. If not, men are not yet free.'

Tidak may occur in other positions than before its head for purposes of emphasis.

Akan tetapi lenjap dia tidak.
'But disappear it will not.'

The negative for nouns and nominal constructs is the premodifier bukan.

Makanannja bukan ikan sadja.
'Its food is not fish only.'

...bahwa jang mereka pimpin itu bukan satu rombongan kambing
'...that those whom they send are not a herd of goats'

Meskipun Kepala Negara tidak bertanggung djawab kepada Dewan Perwakilan Rakjat, ia bukan "diktator" artinja kekuasaan tidak tak terbatas.
'Although the Chief of State is not responsible to the Council of Representatives of the People, he is not a "dictator" in the sense that his power is not unlimited.'

Modal asing bukan Belanda
'Non-Dutch foreign capital'

Tapi bukan itu jang penting.
'But it is not that which is important.'

Bukan main.
'No fooling. Really.'

Bukan also negates or, rather, contradicts any construct, denoting that the circumstances referred to are not true; a statement of the true circumstances usually occurs or is strongly implied.

Sembojan Indonesia Merdeka bukan sekarang sadja kita siarkan. Berpuluh-puluh tahun jang lalu, kita telah menjiarkan sembojan Indonesia Merdeka.
'It is not only now that we have used the slogan "A Free Indonesia." Tens of years ago we were already using the slogan "A Free Indonesia."'

Bukan didalam tahun 1933, tetapi didalam tahun 1921 dan 1922.
'It was not in the year 1933, but in the years 1921 and 1922.'

Bukan seratus lima puluh rupiah harga sehelai kulit dipasar, melainkan...hanja satu rupiah!
'It is not so that one hundred and fifty rupiahs is the price of a sheet of leather at the market, but rather...only one rupiah!'

Bukan is also used as the tag question form in Indonesian, and is appended, after pause and with question intonation, to statements in cases where a confirmation of the content of the statement is requested.

Ini suatu hal jang agak mengherankan, bukan?
'This is a matter which is rather amazing, is it not?'

Tapi dusta banjak, bukan?
'But there's a lot of lying, isn't there?'

The negative for imperative forms is djangan; it functions, however, less like a premodifier than like an imperative form of a verb, and so it is discussed under the imperative (Section 4.4).

For the negative belum, see the following section.

3.3.1.2 Certain premodifiers can be described as aspectual, because they indicate either completeness of continuation.

The premodifier _sudah_ indicates completeness, and so is frequently used to specify that the predicate refers to the past.

Dia pergi.
'He goes (past, present, or future).'

Dia sudah pergi.
'He has already gone; he went.'

Sudah is not premodified by the negative _tidak_. Instead, the form _belum_ occurs. _Belum_ functions syntactically in much the same way as _tidak_.

Dia tidak pergi.
'He doesn't go (past, present, or future).'

Dia belum pergi.
'He has not gone yet; he did not go, but it is expected he will.'

Of course _tidak_ and _sudah_ can occur together, but in that case, neither modifies the other; rather, _sudah_ modifies a predicative which is already modified by _tidak_.

Dia sudah tidak berkerdja lagi.
'He is already out of work again.'

Apabila Soekarno sudah tidak ada lagi,
'When Sukarno has already ceased to exist,'

The premodifier _telah_ also indicates completeness, and is parallel in meaning to _sudah_, from which it differs chiefly by being more formal. It is therefore more commonly found in written and formal spoken material; some authors prefer _telah_, others _sudah_, others use both in the same text, seemingly interchangeably.

Masa telah masak.
'The time is already ripe.'

Dan kita sekarang telah mengindjak 17 Agustus 1960.
'And now we have already arrived at August 17, 1960.'

The premodifier pernah is used to specify that the event referred to by the predicate takes place at least once.

Barangsiapa pernah mentjoba memegang badjing liar, pasti pernah djuga merasai betapa tadjamnja sendjata-sendjata badjing itu.
'Anyone who has ever tried to catch a wild squirrel must also have felt how great is the sharpness of the squirrel's weapons.'

Trotski pernah meneriakkan bahwa partai tidak bisah bersalah...
'Trotski once asserted loudly that the party could not be wrong...'

Pernah may be modified by tidak; the combination means 'at no time, never.'

Maka Marx tidak pernah memikirkan untuk menjusun sebuah filsafah...
'Marx never thought of developing a Philosophy...'

Tak pernah dalam sedjarah pernah terlihat...
'Never in history was there ever seen...'

Pernah may also be modified by belum; the combination means 'never until now, never yet'.

Saja belum pernah kesana.
'I have never yet been there.'

Pernah may also modify the entire sentence structure on occasion.

Perna dia berkata...
'Once he said...'

Pada tahun 1952 pernah pimpinan angkatan perang memohon kepada Presiden...
'On one occasion in 1952 representatives of the armed forces asked the President...'

The premodifiers _tengah_, _sedang_, _masih_ and _lagi_ indicate continuation, and so are frequently used to specify that the predicate refers to a situation which is or was continuing.

They are not, however, completely interchangeable in all situations, and _tengah_ and _lagi_ are of notably less frequent occurrence than _sedang_ and _masih_, respectively.

Dia sedang makan.
'He is eating.'

Dia masih makan.
'He is (still) eating.'

Dia lagi makan.
'He is (still) eating.'

Dia tidak sedang makan.
'He is not eating.'

Saja telah berdjoang dimasa jang lalu dan saja masih berdjoang sekarang.
'I have been a fighter in the past and I am still a fighter now.'

Atau kelas-kelas sedang dalam proses likwidasi.
'Or the classes are now in the process of liquidation.'

Aliran ekonomi-politik Inggris sedang berada pada puntjak kedjajaan mereka.
'The economic-political surge of the English was then at the peak of its greatness.'

3.3.1.3 There is a considerable number of premodifiers which may, because of their meanings, be named intensifiers. The following are examples of this type.

agak	'rather'
amat	'very'
begitu	'so'
berapa	'how much'
hampir	'almost'
kurang	'less'
lebih	'more'
makin	'increasingly'
sangat	'completely
sedikit	'a little'
segala	'completely'
serba	'wholly'
tambah	'more'
terlalu	'too much'
tjukup	'enough'

Memang kita ini belum tjukup matang, memang kita ini masih sedikit Inlander.
'We are certainly not yet mature enough, we are certainly still somewhat bumpkins.'

Djiwa Revolusi sudah mendjadi hampir padam.
'The Spirit of the Revolution is already almost extinguished.'

...adalah amat-amat penting sekali.
'...is very, very important indeed.'

...hanja sedikit mengenal falsafah.
'...were only slightly familiar with philosophy.'

Arti falsafah ini amat sangat ketjil sekali.
'The meaning of the philosophy was very scant.'

...tidak berpikir lebih djauh.
'...did not think any further.'

Malah perdjoangan berdjalan laksana lawine jang makin lama makin gemuruh.
'But the struggle moves like an avalanche, the longer it continues, the more thunderous it becomes.'

3.3.1.4 The premodifier hanja 'only' premodifies constructs of any description. It is increasingly used in connection with the postmodifier sadja,'only'. Some speakers claim that there is a difference in meaning between the two forms, but it is a tenuous difference at best; for all practical purposes the two forms are the same; certainly where both modify the same form there is no observable difference between them.

Mereka hanja sanggup menjatakannja setjara passif.
'They are only capable of manifesting it in a passive manner.'

Hanja dengan kooperasi dapat dibangan kemakmuran rakjat.
'Only with co-operation can the prosperity of the people be built up.'

Hanja satu jang sulit untuk mentjari kontak ialah dengan AU.
'The only one which was difficult to contact was the Air Force.'

Saja hanja menjebutkan jang terpenting sadja.
'I only mention the most important.'

The premodifier salah premodifies only the number satu or se-, 'one'; salah is emphatic.

Djiwa Gotong Rojong adalah salah satu tjorak daripada Kepribadian Indonesia.
'The spirit of Gotong Rojong is but one feature of the Individuality of Indonesia.'

3.3.1.5 Some of the intensifiers already mentioned, as well as certain other premodifiers, occur also as postmodifiers of predicatives. Among those which may occur both as premodifiers and postmodifiers are included

amat	'very'
sangat	'completely'
sedikit	'a little'.

Forms which occur only as postmodifiers are

benar	'truly'
betul	'truly'
sekali	'very'
lagi	'again, more'
pula	'again, in return'.

The _lagi_ which postmodifies predicatives is different from the _lagi_ which premodifies predicatives. The postmodifier has a meaning of 'again' or 'more', while the premodifier has the meaning of 'still' or 'continually'.

...jang berbahaja sekali
'...which is very dangerous'

...bahwa sistim-sistim falsafah tidak ada lagi dan gunanja.
'...that the systems of philosophy no longer had any meaning or use to them.'

Itu perlu benar.
'This is truly necessary.'

Demokrasi desa jang begitu kuat hidupnja adalah pula dasar bagi pemerintahan.
'The democracy of the village, which is so strong in its vitality, is, in addition, a basis for a form of government.'

Of the postmodifiers given above, _pula_ especially differs from the others in that it may either postmodify the entire predicative construct or the first item in the construct. In the cases where the head of the predicative construct is preceded by an auxiliary or premodifier, pula may occur after the auxiliary or premodifier.

Tidak pula diadakan pemungutan suara...
'Moreover, there is no counting of votes.'

Harus pula dialami hidjrah ke Barat.
'In addition, the settling of the West had to be undertaken.'

The postmodifier sadja postmodifies any construct, and functions like the premodifier hanja except for its positional relationship to the head which it modifies. It is most frequently used in formal writing in connection with hanja or with bukan or tidak to form a coordinating construct, but there are cases where it is used without these.

Revolusi itu bukanlah kerdja satu golongan sadja.
'These revolutions were not the work of one faction only.'

Saja diam sadja.
'I just kept silent.'

3.3.1.6 Also to be included in the class of postmodifiers are the enclitics -lah, -kah, -pun.

The enclitic -lah is a predicate marker. It can be added to any predicative or auxiliary or modifier; it can also be added to a nominal construct if the nominal construct forms the predicate of the sentence or participates in it.

The enclitic -lah may occur with the first item of the predicate when the subject precedes the predicate, but is complex (particularly when it contains predicatives) or potentially ambiguous.

Anggota-anggota Dewan Perwakilan Rakjat jang pertama kali mewakili seluruh Indonesia menurut

Undang-Undang Dasar 1950 bukanlah anggota jang dipilih oleh rakjat.
'The members of the People's Representative Council who for the first time represented all Indonesia in accordance with the Constitution of 1950 were not members who were chosen by the people.'

The enclitic -lah may occur when the predicate precedes the subject, particularly if the predicate is not otherwise marked.

Maka timbullah krisis kabinet.
'A cabinet crisis developed.'

Hari ini Presiden Soekarno-lah jang berbitjara dihadapan tuan-tuan.
'Today it is President Soekarno who is speaking before you.'

Demikianlah Pantja Sila kami.
'Such are our Five Principles.'

Kalau ia tidak dapat menemuinja, nistjaja akan dipotong oranglah kepalanja.
'If he is not able to discover it, his head will certainly be cut off.'

The enclitic -lah may also occur where only a part of the predicate precedes the subject. It is then postposed to the last item of the part of the predicate which precedes the subject.

Disanalah kami menghadapi imperialisme dan kekuatan bersendjata dari imperialisme.
'There we faced imperialism and the armed force of imperialism.'

The enclitic -lah tends to occur when there is no subject, and the predicate begins the sentence.

Bukanlah pion-pion diatas papan tjatur jang tuan-tuan hadapi.
'It is not pawns on a chess board you are dealing

with.'

In imperative sentences, when there may frequently be no subject, the enclitic -lah is postposed to the imperative form, especially in the case where the form is possibly ambiguous. Apart from marking the imperative form in this way, -lah is sometimes said to introduce a note of suggestion rather than of command, and to modify the possible brusqueness of the command so that it becomes a polite request.

Bangkitlah kembali! ...Tinggalkan alam jang lampau!... Berbesarlah hati bahwa kita sekarang ini sadar, dan berdjalanlah terus!
'Rise again! Leave the realm of the past! Be proud that we are now aware, and forge ahead!'

Lihat, lihatlah delegasi jang mendukung saja!
'Look, just look at the delegation which supports me!'

Idjinkanlah saja sekarang beralih kemasalah jang lebih luas.
'Permit me now to go on to a broader problem.'

Akan tetapi marilah kami realistis.
'However, let us be realistic.'

The enclitic -kah indicates that a sentence is interrogative. This enclitic may occur with any item of the sentence, even with a word which is itself interrogative. Since -kah tends to focus attention on, and to emphasize, the word to which it is attached, there is also a marked tendency for that word to occur at the beginning of the sentence or clause, if the construct in which it functions will permit such an arrangement.

Tertjapaikah atau tidak kemakmuran rakjat...?
'Is it achieved or not, this prosperity of the people...?'

Tidakkah pula Hitler demikian?
'Was not Hitler, moreover, such a man?'

...mana jang Tuan-tuan pilih: trisila, ekasila ataukah pantjasila?
'...which is it that you will choose: a set of three principles, a set of one, or a set of five?'

...dilapangan politikkah, dilapangan ekonomikah, dilapangan militerkah...
'...whether in the area of politics, in the area of economics, or in the military sphere...'

Apakah tudjuan kita djangka-pendek, dan apa tudjuan kita djangka-pandjang itu?
'What are our short-term plans and what are our long-term plans?'

Siapakah diantara tuan-tuan menolak Pantja Sila?
'Who among you rejects the Five Principles?'

Bagaimanakah penggunaan setjara internasional daripada Pantja Sila?
'What kind of international advantage can be derived from the Five Principles?'

Potlotmukah ini jang ketinggalan dimedja?
'Is this your pencil that has been left on the table?'

Bukankah begitu, teman-temanku?
'Is it not so, my friends?'

The enclitic -pun serves to emphasize the item to which it is added; usually the emphasized item occurs as close to the beginning of the sentence as its construct will permit. In the orthography, -pun is usually written as one word with the preceding word, but this is not always the case; -lah and -kah are always joined to the preceding item.

Pembangunan demokrasi pun terlantar karena pertjektjokan politik senantiasa.
'The development of even our democracy is neglected because of the continuous political squabbling.'

Undang-undang Dasar Negara manapun tidak dapat dimengerti, kalau hanja dibatja tekstnja sadja.
'No Constitution whatsoever can be understood only by reading its text.'

Djelas disinipun sudah ta'boleh diberi djalan kepada ekonomi liberal.
'It is clear right here that it is already impossible to take the road towards a liberal economic system.'

regime jang barupun
'even a new regime' or 'a regime, however new'

--dibawah bendera ideologi apapun djuga, atau dibawah tenaga sosial apa djuga--
'--under the flag of any ideology whatsoever, or under any social control whatever--'

The enclitic -pun is a component of certain conjunctions such as maupun and meskipun; in such cases its emphatic force is not always readily apparent.

3.3.1.7 The modifier djuga 'also' modifies any construct, either as a premodifier or a postmodifier.

Tesis ini djuga sebahagian sadja benar.
'This thesis also is only in part true.'

Djuga didalam urusan kepala negara
'Also in the office of the chief of state'

3.4 Ordinators

Ordinators are of three types: coordinators, connectives (Section 3.5) and subordinators

(Section 3.6).

3.4.1 Coordinators

Coordinators connect a syntactic unit or construct of any kind--from a single word through a complete sentence structure--with another unit or construct which has the same syntactic function. The structures coordinated in this way function as one syntactic unit.

Single coordinators occur between the structures being coordinated. If more than two structures are coordinated, the coordinator may occur between all possible pairs of items, or only between the last pair. In the latter case, features of pause and intonation in speech, and commas in the orthography, will indicate the bounds of the structures being coordinated.

Correlated coordinators occur in two segments; the first segment precedes the first structure to be correlated, and the second segment precedes the second structure. If more than two structures are correlated, the first segment usually precedes each structure but the last, and the second segment precedes the last structure.

The single coordinators are:

dan	'and'
tetapi, tapi	'but'
atau	'or'
maupun	'and'

Tetapi may be preceded by _akan_.

Beberapa ekor ajam, itik dan telur.
'A few chickens, ducks and eggs.'

Monjet adalah binatang jang mendatangkan rugi dan jang berguna bagi hutan.

'The monkey is an animal which causes damage to and which is beneficial to the forest.'

...jang dapat diberikan kepada dan dipunjai oleh orang-orang...
'...which can be accorded to and possessed by persons...'

Hal ini benar, akan tetapi tidak seluruhnja.
'This statement is true, but not completely.'

Suatu masa besar dilahirkan abad ,
Tetapi masa besar itu menemui manusia ketjil.
'A mighty epoch has this century brought forth,
But the great moment finds but a puny breed.'

--asing atau bukan asing--
'--foreigner or no--'

Sudah banjak orang-hutan jang ditangkap atau ditembak orang.
'There are already many orangutans which are captured or shot by people.'

Ia bebas dari pendjadjahan asing dalam rupa apapun djuga, politik maupun ideologi.
'It will be free of foreign influence of any sort whatever, whether political or ideological.'

Sometimes other forms are used in cases where <u>dan</u> may also occur. Of these the more notable are <u>dengan</u>, <u>sama</u> and <u>lagi</u>.

Siti dengan Amat
'Siti and Amat'

Saja sama Ali
'Ali and I'

Djari-djari kaki itu seakan-akan djari-djari pajung, pandjang lagi tipis.
'These toes are very much like the ribs of an umbrella, long and thin.'

The correlated coordinators are:

baik...maupun	'either, or; not only, but also'
tidak...(akan) tetapi	'not...but'
bukan...(akan) tetapi	'not...but'
tidak...melainkan	'not...but'
bukan...melainkan	'not...but'

baik didalam maupun diluar Konstituante
'either in the Constituent Assembly or out of it'

Pasal-pasal, baik jang hanja mengenai warga negara maupun jang mengenai seluruh penduduk...
'The articles, both those which only affect citizens and those which affect all residents...'

Sistim demokrasi-liberal tidak hanja merupakan suatu halangan, tapi djuga merupakan suatu bahaja bagi kelandjutan Revolusi kita.
'The liberal-democratic system not only constitutes an obstacle, but also constitutes a danger to the advancement of our Revolution.'

Achirnja orang masuk partai bukan karena kejakinan, melainkan karena ingin memperoleh djaminan.
'Finally, people join a party not because of conviction, but because they want to obtain the benefits.'

Structures are also frequently arranged in parataxis, that is, are simply arranged one after another with no coordinators between; many sentences have a number of predicates paratactically arranged rather than having some subordinated to others with conjunctions.

Sepatah dua patah kata
'One or two words'

...jang sekarang berubah mendjadi Dewan Pertimbangan Agung...
'...which has changed and become the Supreme

Council for Review...'

Saja akan berusaha tidak akan menambah serta tidak akan mengurangi apa jang saja saksikan.
'I am going to try not to add to and likewise not to subtract from that which I am reporting.'

3.5 Connectives

The connective _maka_ introduces a sentence structure to indicate that the sentence structure which it introduces is not subordinated to any other sentence, but is independent. Thus, in a group of sentence structures, some of which are subordinate, _maka_ serves to mark the sentence structure to which the others are to be subordinated. It occurs most frequently when the subordinate clauses precede the independent clause.

Sesudah saja bitjarakan tentang hal "merdeka", maka sekarang saja bitjarakan tentang hal dasar.
'I have finished discussing the question of "freedom", and now I shall discuss the question of principles.'

Menurut geopolitik, maka Indonesialah tanah-air kita.
'According to geopolitics, it is Indonesia which is our homeland.'

Apabila Dewan Perwakilan Rakjat tidak menjetudjui anggaran jang diusulkan Pemerintah, maka Pemerintah mendjalankan anggaran tahun jang lalu.
'When the Council of the People's Representatives shall not have agreed on the budget which is proposed by the Government, then the Government shall implement the budget of the preceding year.'

Maka also occurs initially in a sentence to indicate both that the clause it introduces is an independent clause and also that it follows from, but is not dependent on, the previous sentence.

Maka timbullah anarki dalam politik dan ekonomi.
'Then there will arise anarchy in the political field and in the economic.'

A similar function can also be fulfilled by certain other items, particularly by the coordinators.

Dan orang tjoba membuat konsepsi demokrasi Indonesia jang moderen.
'And people try to utilize the modern concept of Indonesian democracy.'

Tetapi sedjarah memberi peladjaran djuga pada manusia.
'But history brings knowledge also to mankind.'

Bahkan saja berkata lebih lagi dari itu.
'Moreover, I will say more than that.'

Malah tjara-tjara jang demikian itu ternjata makin mengkotjar-katjirkan dan membentjanai revolusi.
'On the contrary, such things clearly only confuse and disturb the revolution the more.'

3.6 Subordinators

Subordinators are of two types: prepositions and conjunctions.

A preposition unites with a following noun or nominal structure to form an exocentric construct which functions as a modifier. These prepositional constructs usually modify predicatives, but may, on occasion, modify nouns or nominal structures.

A conjunction unites with a following sentence structure to form an exocentric construct. This type of construct, which is here called a subordinate clause, functions as a modifier. Most subordinate clauses modify predicatives, but some modify nominal structures or function as nominal structures.

3.6.1 Prepositions

Prepositions constitute a distinct class of subordinators in modern Indonesian. However, in the earlier stages of the language, it is probable that the class of prepositions was much smaller. Contact with other languages which have a category of prepositions has gradually introduced more prepositional forms into Indonesian; some of these were clearly borrowed from those other languages; some were composed of Indonesian elements.

Indeed, it is still easy to imagine that many of the prepositions, which have the same form as predicative or nominal roots, were originally predicates governing dependencies and coordinated in series with other predicates.

Because of this process of development, there is a certain amount of fluctuation in usage among various speakers.

The outstanding case of such fluctuation and borrowing in contemporary Indonesian is to be found in the forms corresponding to the English 'without'; there is a series of expressions of diverse origin with little consistency among their use, in cases, even on the part of one speaker or writer. The following forms are found, though not all are common.

zonder	'without' (from Dutch)
tanpa	'without' (from Javanese)
tidak dengan	('not with')
dengan tidak ada	('with there is not')
tidak ada	('there is not')
tidak pakai	('not use')
tanpa dengan	('without with')

Sometimes the need for the preposition is circumvented entirely. Thus, 'tea without sugar' may be teh tidak pakai gula ('tea not use sugar') or, more simply, teh pahit ('bitter tea').

While certain prepositions are used consistently by most speakers of Indonesian, then, others may fluctuate in their usage, depending upon the speaker's language background, level of education in general, and exposure to foreign languages in particular.

The simplest manner of defining the members of the class of prepositions is to list them. Such a list may, however, be incomplete for certain speakers, and may include items which other speakers normally avoid.

3.6.1.1 The following is a list of the commoner Indonesian prepositions, with an approximate indication of their meaning.

The Basic Prepositions:

di-	'in, at'
ke-	'to, towards'
dari	'from'

Other Prepositions:

akan	'involving'
bagi	'for the sake of'
buat	'for the use of'
demi	'by'
dengan	'with'
guna	'for the sake of'
oleh	'by the agency of'
sampai	'as far as, until'
tanpa	'without'
tentang	'concerning'
untuk	'for the benefit of'

There is also a considerable number of prepositions which are morphologically complex, being most frequently formed by the prefix se- and some other element. Examples are:

setjara	'in the manner of'
sebelum	'before (in time)'
selama	'as long as (in time)'
setelah	'after (in time)'

The following is a list of examples of these various kinds of preposition:

oleh Presiden Soekarno
'by President Sukarno'

dengan djiwa jang murni
'with a pure spirit'

bagi manusia biasa
'for the common man'

penjataan tentang Pantjasila sebagai filsafat atau ideologi negara
'a declaration about the Five Principles as a national philosophy or ideology'

baik bagi rakjat dan masjarakat
'good for the people and for the society'

oleh sebab itu
'for this reason'

demonstrasi setjara damai
'a peaceful demonstration'

dari daerah kekuasaan radja
'out of the area of the king's authority'

pemerintahan dari jang diperintah
'government (derives) from the governed'

perlu akan suatu pemerintah jang kuat
'need a strong government'

selama masa ini
'during this time'

Pantjasila sebagai filsafat atau ideologi negara
'The Five Principles as a national philosophy or ideology'

Other forms, which are clearly composed of a root with affixes, may be interpreted either as prepositions or as predicatives paratactically coordinated.

menurut	'according to'
melawan	'against'

Menurut kaum revolusioner model lama
'According to the old-style revolutionaries'

Orang Polandia berontak melawan Prusia.
'The people of Poland rose against Prussia.'

3.6.1.2 The three basic prepositions, <u>di</u>-, <u>ke</u>- and <u>dari</u>-, combine with certain nouns to provide a variety of complex prepositions which, for the most part, form adverbials of place. These nouns will be called here locational nouns. Examples of such nouns are:

atas	'topside'
bawah	'underside'
depan	'front'
muka	'front, face'
belakang	'back'
sebelah	'side'
antara	'middle'
dalam	'inside'
luar	'outside'

seberang	'the other side'
hadapan	'a position facing'

Examples of the combinations are:

diatas medja	'on the table'
keatas medja	'onto the table'
dari atas medja	'off the table'
didalam rumah	'in the house'
disebelah rumah	'beside the house'
kedalam rumah	'into the house'
kebelakang rumah	'to the back of the house'
dari luar rumah	'from outside the house'
dari seberang sungai	'from the other side of the river'

Tak seorangpun diantara kita
'No person among us'

Saja berbitjara dihadapan para pemimpin bangsa-bangsa.
'I am speaking before the representatives of the various countries.'

Didalam desa-desa	'In the villages'
Dibawah feodalisme	'Under feudalism'
Didalam tulisan saja	'In my writings'

Certain of the locational nouns may occur with or without the preposition <u>di</u>-. In those cases where <u>di</u>- may or may not occur, but does not, these nouns, in effect, function as prepositions.

dalam dunia bukan-komunis
'in the non-communist world'

terdiri atas dua fondamen
'is based on two fundamental principles'

persaudaraan antara manusia
'brotherhood among men'

Conversely, in cases where the positional relationship is obvious, the locational noun may not occur.

diatas medja	'on the table'
dimedja	'on the table'
didalam lemari	'in the cupboard'
dilemari	'in the cupboard'

Naturally, if some other positional relationship is intended than the obvious one of 'on the top surface of the table' or 'in the interior of the cupboard', then this relationship must be specified by means of a locational noun.

The expression dirumah usually means 'at home', 'in or about the house', in contrast with didalam rumah which means specifically 'inside the house'.

Contemporary Indonesian uses the basic prepositions directly with the names of cities, countries, islands, continents and so on. The older use, which is still found, avoids using the prepositions directly before such names, but uses instead a generic noun between the preposition and the name.

ke Semarang	'to Semarang'
kekota Semarang	'to Semarang'
di Inggeris	'in England'
dinegeri Inggeris	'in England'
dari Djawa	'from Java'
dari pulau Djawa	'from Java'

3.6.1.3 A special type of locational noun is pada; there is no satisfactory means of indicating its meaning, though such a translation as 'immediate vicinity' is somewhat indicative. Pada is used when the following noun designates a human being, or when the noun designates an abstraction, so that the idea of location is highly figurative; it is consistently used with persons, but the more figurative cases exhibit a certain amount of variation from speaker to speaker.

The preposition _di_ does not occur with _pada_, so that _pada_ alone occurs where _di_ would otherwise be expected. The preposition _ke_ does occur regularly with _pada_. The preposition _dari_ freely occurs either with _pada_ or without it, except in certain specific cases, such as in the comparison of adjectives, where _daripada_ always occurs.

pada saja	'on me'
kepada saja	'to me'
dari saja	'from me'
daripada saja	'from me'

Ia lebih tinggi daripada saja.
'He is taller than I.'

Fakta-fakta akan lebih dapat berbitjara daripada manusianja sendiri.
'The facts will be better able to speak than the people themselves.'

Pada is also employed in expressions of time.

pada bulan Agustus	'in the month of August'
pada tahun 1945	'in 1945'

The various uses of _pada_, _kepada_ and _daripada_ are difficult to define because of the degree of fluctuation among various speakers.

Whereas, in the orthography, _dari_ is not commonly written as one word with the succeeding noun, in the case of _daripada_ it is becoming more usual to write the combination as one word.

3.6.1.4 The preposition sampai may occur with the preposition di- or the preposition ke-, to form a compound preposition which has much the same meaning as the prepositions without sampai.

sampai di lobang kubur
'until the grave'

dari Sabang, sampai ke Merauke
'from Sabang to Merauke'; 'all Indonesia'

It also occurs with dengan with the meaning 'up to and including'.

dari tanggal 10 Djuni 1945 sampai dengan tanggal 17 Djuli 1945.
'From June 10, 1945 to July 17, 1945 inclusive.'

3.6.1.5 When a preposition governs a pronoun, if the pronoun has an enclitic form, the enclitic may be used as the object of the preposition; the enclitic is not used, however, directly with the proclitic prepositions di- or ke-.

padaku	'on me'
olehmu	'by you'
kepadanja	'to him'

siapa jang lebih taqwa kepadaKu
'whoever is most devoted to Me'

3.6.1.6 It has been said above that all prepositions govern a following nominal construct. Certain of the prepositions readily govern verbal structures as well, but since these can possibly be interpreted as nominalized verbs (Section 3.1.6.2), they will be described here in that way. It should be noted that when a verb is nominalized, it may continue to govern its dependency in a normal fashion.

Dengan lewatnja waktu
'With the passing of time'

Dengan tiada berbuat apa-apa
'Without doing anything'

Untuk mengurangi bahaja itu
'In order to lessen this danger'

Kami berhak untuk didengar.
'We have a right to be heard.'

3.6.2 Conjunctions

Conjunctions, like prepositions, constitute a nebulous but growing form class in Indonesian. It is even clearer in the case of conjunctions than of prepositions that Indonesian originally did not use conjunctions extensively, but tended rather simply to juxtapose sentences in such a way that the relationships indicated in certain other languages by conjunctions were clearly implied. As contact with other languages developed, the use of conjunctions developed; some conjunctions are clearly borrowed from Sanskrit, others from Arabic. There are, in consequence, a number of conjunctions which appear to be synonymous with other conjunctions. An overall consistency in the use of the conjunctions is yet to be achieved.

It is characteristic of all conjunctions that they govern a sentence construct as a dependency, and that they do not participate in the structure of the sentence they govern, except for jang, which functions as the subject or topic of the sentence it governs.

A conjunction and the sentence structure it governs together form an exocentric construct which has a syntactic function as part of another sentence structure. Such an exocentric construct is called a subordinate clause. Subordinate clauses may function either as modifiers of sentence structures, or as nominals.

The simplest means of defining the class of conjunctions is by listing all of the conjunctions. Such a list may, however, be incomplete for certain speakers, and may include items which other speakers normally avoid.

3.6.2.1 The following conjunctions form subordinate clauses which function as sentence modifiers for the most part.

Conjunctions of Time:

sebelum	'before'
sesudah	'after'
setelah	'after'
sedjak	'since'
semendjak	'since'
ketika	'when'
tatkala	'when'
waktu	'when'
apabila	'when'
bilamana	'when'
sedang	'while'
sedangkan	'while'
sementara	'while'
sambil	'while'
selama	'during'

Other conjunctions:

djika	'if, provided that'
kalau	'if, provided that'
djikalau	'if, provided that'
seandainja	'if, provided that'
kalau-kalau	'if, provided that'
umpamanja	'if, provided that'
andaikata	'if, provided that'
asal	'if, provided that'
asalkan	'if, provided that'

agar	'in order to'
supaja	'in order to'
agar supaja	'in order to'

biarpun	'although'
meskipun	'although'
sekalipun	'although'
sungguhpun	'although'
walaupun	'although'
seakan-akan	'as if'
seolah-olah	'as if'
sebagaimana	'as, like'
seperti	'as, like'
sebagai	'as, like'
laksana	'as, like'
sebab	'because'
karena	'because'
hingga	'to the point that'
sehingga	'to the point that'
sampai	'to the point that'

Sebelum negara merdeka, maka harus lebih dahulu ini selesai, itu selesai...
'Before the state becomes independent, it would be better first to do this, to finish that...'

Sedang masih berlaku revolusi, kaum komunis menghantjurkan hak-milik kapitalis...
'While the revolution was still going on, the communists smashed the rights of ownership of the capitalists...'

Demokrasi dapat berdjalan baik, apabila ada rasa tanggung djawab dan toleransi pada pemimpin-pemimpin politik.
'Democracy can function well when there is a feeling of responsibility and tolerance among the political representatives.'

Kemakmuran rakjat jang ditjita-tjitakan masih djauh sadja, sedangkan nilai uang makin merosot.
'That prosperity of the people which has been held up as an ideal is still far off, while the value

of the money has steadily declined.'

Lihatlah pula--djikalau tuan-tuan kehendaki tjontoh jang lebih hebat--Sovjet Rusia!
'Or consider again--if you want a more striking example--Soviet Russia!'

Kaum buruh setjara tak langsung mendjadi milik golongan itu, meskipun tak sepenuhja dimikian, karena buruh adalah pula seorang manusia individuil.
'Labor, in an indirect fashion, becomes a chattel of this group, although this is not entirely the case, because each laborer is nonetheless an individual human being.'

Supaja berkehidupan kebangsaan jang bebas, maka rakjat Indonesia menjatakan dengan ini kemerdekaanja.
'In order that it may live the life of a free nation, the people of Indonesia declares with these presents its independence.'

...dilakukan dengan rasa tanggung djawab, agar terlaksana keadilan sosial.
'...is done with a sense of responsibility in order that social justice may be achieved.'

3.6.2.2 The conjunction which forms subordinate clauses that function as nominals, and which does not participate in the structure of the clause it introduces is:

bahwa 'that'

The conjunction bahwa may occur or not occur when the clause which it introduces is the object of a verb. When the clause is the subject of the sentence, or the predicate, or in apposition to a noun, however, bahwa does occur.

Mereka berkata, bahwa kita tidak boleh merobah negara federal.

'They said that we were not permitted to change the federal state.'

Kita merasakan bahwa pertumbuhan atau kemadjuan kurang lantjar.
'We feel that our growth or progress is not going smoothly enough.'

Djelas bahwa autoriteit tertinggi ini bukan orang...
'It is clear that this highest authority is not one man...'

Bahwa Soekarno seorang patriot jang tjinta pada Tanah Airnja, dan ingin melihat Indonesia jang adil dan makmur selekas-lekasnja, itu tidak dapat disangkal.
'That Sukarno is a patriot who loves his native land, and wishes to see a just and prosperous Indonesia as quickly as possible, this cannot be denied.'

Salah satu dari kesulitan jang terutama ialah bahwa tjita-tjita demokrasi memang ada di Indonesia.
'One of the most outstanding of these difficulties is that the ideal of democracy certainly exists in Indonesia.'

Dan disitu pulalah terletak djaminan, bahwa demokrasi tidak akan lenjap di Indonesia.
'And here once again can be given assurance that democracy will not disappear in Indonesia.'

3.6.2.3 The conjunction which forms subordinate clauses functioning as nominals, and which does participate in the structure of the clause it introduces, acting as the subject or topic of the clause, is

jang	'(the one) who, which, that, etc.'

Sentence structures introduced by _jang_ as the subject do not have, except under the most exceptional circumstances, a nominal as a predicate.

Marxisme jang tak bisa membuat kesalahan
'Marxism, which can do no wrong'

Unsur jang paling djahat menurut pandangan pekerdja jang terdapat didalam kapitalisme kuno...
'The factor that, from the point of view of the workers, was most evil in classical capitalism...'

Apa jang terdjadi sekarang ialah KRISIS dari pada demokrasi.
'That which is happening now is a CRISIS of democracy.'

Bagi saja jang lama bertengkar dengan Soekarno...
'For me who have long disputed with Sukarno...'

Dalam politik hak seseorang sama dengan jang lain.
'In politics the rights of one man are the same as those of the others.'

Siapa jang berani menjangkal bangsa, jang melahirkan dia?
'Who is there who is so bold as to deny the country which gave him birth?'

The stricture that _jang_ must serve as the subject or topic of the sentence structure which it introduces and in which it participates is commonly observed in contemporary Indonesian. In cases where _jang_ would be the object of an active transitive verb, the verb is made passive, whereupon _jang_ becomes the subject.

Oleh karena itu jang kami bitjarakan dalam buku ini ialah binatang-binatang jang terdapat di Indonesia.
'For this reason, what we are going to discuss in

this book is the animals which are to be found in Indonesia.'

Monopoli hak-milik jang mereka pegang.
'The monopoly of the right of ownership which they hold (which is held by them).'

Occasionally such passive constructions do not show the strict word order which is usually found in passive sentences, in that the agent and the verb form may be separated by other structural items.

hanja Indonesia seluruhnja, jang telah berdiri didjaman Sri Widjaja dan Madjapahit dan jang kini pula kita harus dirikan.
'only Indonesia in its entirety, which has already been in existence in the times of Sri Widjaja and Madjapahit, and which again must be established by us now.'

Under the influence of foreign languages, particularly the Western European languages, there has occasionally been a tendency to construct sentence structures of this type in which jang was the object of a verb or of a preposition. This is definitely a foreign effect, however, and such structures would ordinarily be rearranged in such a way as to ensure that jang becomes the subject.

Jang saja maksud ialah Aldjazair.
'What I have in mind is Algeria.'

Jang may also serve as the topic of the sentence in which it participates.

Hendaknja negara Indonesia ialah negara jang tiap-tiap orangnja dapat menjembah Tuhannja dengan tjara jang leluasa.
'It is to be hoped that the state of Indonesia is a state whose every citizen can worship his God in a manner which is at his own discretion.'

Orang-orang jang djiwanja "mandek".
'People whose spirit has "come to a standstill".'

Mendirikan negara Indonesia Merdeka jang namanja sadja Indonesia Merdeka?
'To set up a country, Free Indonesia, which is Free Indonesia in name only?'

Kera mempunjai ekor pandjang jang gunanja untuk mendjaga keseimbangan kalau memandjat.
'The monkey has a long tail whose purpose is to maintain his balance if he is climbing.'

Pinggangnja diikat dengan tali pandjang jang udjungnja dipegang oleh jang menjuruh itu.
'Its waist is tied by a long cord whose end is held by the one who controls it.'

In some cases, jang is used as a topic, followed first by the subject and then by the active verb conjoined with the enclitic pronoun -nja; this is an unusual variation of the typical topic-comment sentence structure, in which it is the subject which has the enclitic -nja; such structures are rather rare, but they provide another manner of avoiding the situation where jang becomes the object in the clause it introduces.

Kita mendirikan negara Indonesia, jang kita semua harus mendukungnja.
'We are building the Indonesian state which we must all support.'

kemakmuran rakjat jang Soekarno sendiri djuga mentjiptakannja dengan sepenuh-penuh fantasinja?
'that prosperity of the people which Sukarno himself dreamed up in the most fantastic way possible?'

In cases where jang would otherwise be the object of a preposition, the most normal rearrangement is to construct two separate and independent sentences. Other arrangements, such as the introduction of the noun tempat, have been cited as possible, but are not actually in wide use.

Sebentar lagi burung-burung itu masuk ke loteng atau kerusuk-rusuk atap rumah tempat ia tidur malam hari.
'A little later these birds enter the attic or the eaves of the roof where they sleep at night.'

However, probably as a result of the writer's knowledge of foreign languages, the form mana, which is basically an interrogative form, is occasionally used after prepositions as the conjunction in a clause of this type.

suatu "Weltanschauung", diatas mana kita mendirikan negara Indonesia itu.
'a "Political Outlook" on the basis of which we will build this state of Indonesia.'

Tahun 1959 adalah tahun dalam mana kita...kembali kepada Undang-undang Dasar 1945.
'The year 1959 is the year in which we...return to the Constitution of 1945.'

Markas KOSTRAD, dimana memang saja bertugas sebagai Panglima KOSTRAD.
'The KOSTRAD army post, where, of course, I had business as the General of KOSTRAD.'

3.6.2.4 Another type of subordinate clause which functions as a nominal construct is the indirect question. The question retains its basic direct form without shifts in word order, and without being introduced by any conjunction. If the direct question does not begin with an interrogative form, -kah is joined to the first word (but not to a preposition); -kah is also added on occasion even to the interrogative words.

Saja mengerti apakah jang Paduka tuan Ketua kehendaki!
'I understand what the honorable chairman wants!'

Jang mereka ketahui, ialah bagaimana merampas kekuasaan atas perekonomian.
'The thing that they know is how to seize control of the economy.'

djika mengetahui kesimpulan-kesimpulan apa jang dibuat orang dari pemikiran-pemikirannja itu.
'if he had known the problems which people were going to create from these ideas of his.'

3.7 Adverbials

Adverbials form a group whose members vary widely in structure, but whose function and distribution are very similar.

Structurally, adverbs may be single words, sometimes distinctive in form, and sometimes having the same form as nouns, verbs, or most particularly, adjectives; adverbials may also be prepositional phrases or subordinate clauses.

Functionally, adverbials modify sentence structures. They most commonly occur after the basic sentence. They may occur before it. They may also, with certain exceptions, occur between the two chief components of the basic sentence structure, that is, between the subject and the predicate. Infrequently they may occur within the predicate structure between a verb and its dependency. These variations in position of occurrence involve differences in emphasis or in style rather than difference in function.

Adverbs can be subdivided into a number of classes on the basis of the particular interrogative form which is associated with each class. Some of these classes are individually useful in a discussion of Indonesian syntax, but others can merely be considered as members of the larger class of adverbials, without a real need for further subdivision. The major classes of adverbials are the adverbials of Time (3.7.1), Place (3.7.2), Manner (3.7.3) and Purpose (3.7.6). Other classes, consisting entirely of prepositional phrases or subordinate clauses, might also be distinguished on the basis of the prepositions or conjunctions which occur, if this should appear to be desirable.

3.7.1 Adverbials of Time

Adverbials of time answer the questions Bilamana? 'When?', Kapan? 'When?', Berapa lama? 'How long?' The forms bilamana and kapan are generally interchangeable; kapan is from Javanese, and is felt to be less formal than bilamana. Questions referring to time can also be framed by introducing interrogative words into prepositional phrases of time, or clauses of time.

pada djam berapa?	'at what hour?'
pada bulan apa?	'in what month?'

Certain adverbials of time are simple words. These include such forms as

kemarin	'yesterday'
besok	'tomorrow'
lusa	'the day after tomorrow'
sekarang	'now'
dulu	'earlier'
tadi	'earlier today'
nanti	'later'
siang	'in the daytime'
pagi	'in the morning'
sore	'in the afternoon'
malam	'at night'

Other adverbials of time are composed of groups of simple words.

kemarin dulu	'the day before yesterday'
nanti malam	'this (coming) evening'
tadi pagi	'this (past) morning'
pagi-pagi	'early in the morning'

Still other adverbials of time are prepositional phrases. The prepositions which occur are

di-	'on, at'
pada	'on, at'
dalam	'in'
dari	'from'
sampai	'until
sampai dengan	'until and including'
selama	'during'
sesudah	'after'
sebelum	'before'
sedjak	'since'
untuk	'for'

There is a group of nouns referring to fixed lengths of time; these may be called generic nouns of time. Typical nouns of this group are:

djam	'hour'
tanggal	'date'
tahun	'year'
hari	'day'
bulan	'month'
malam	'night'

There is another group of nouns which serve as the names for such fixed lengths of time; these may be called the specific nouns of time. The nouns for the days of the week are:

Minggu	'Sunday'
Senin	'Monday'
Selasa	'Tuesday'
Rabo, Rebo	'Wednesday'
Kemis	'Thursday'

Djum'at	'Friday'
Sabtu	'Saturday'

The nouns for the months of the year are:

Djanuari	'January'
Pebruari	'February'
Maret	'March'
April	'April'
Mei	'May'
Djuni	'June'
Djuli	'July'
Agustus	'August'
September	'September'
Oktober	'October'
Nopember	'November'
Desember	'December'

Numerals are used to specify hours, dates, years, and so on.

The generic nouns must be modified when they occur in prepositional phrases. The most frequently occurring modifiers are specific nouns, but other types of modification also occur.

pada djam tiga	'at three o'clock'
pada tanggal 17 Agustus	'on the 17th of August'
pada tahun 1945	'in 1945'
pada hari Selasa	'on Tuesday'
pada bulan Maret	'in March'

Specific nouns of time occur only rarely as objects of prepositions; it is more common that the generic noun precede them in prepositional constructs.

In combinations of time nouns, the date customarily precedes the month, and this precedes the year. The designation of the day precedes the noun designating a portion of the day.

dari tanggal 29 Mei tahun 1945 sampai dengan tanggal 1 Djuni 1945
'from May 29, 1945, to June 1, 1945, inclusive'

pada hari Rabu sore
'on Wednesday evening'

The noun malam, however, may occur either before or after the name of the day, but there is a difference in meaning. Since the day is reckoned as beginning at sunset, malam Saptu ('the night of Saturday') refers to the night which precedes the day Saturday, and so is equivalent to the English 'Friday night'. On the other hand, Saptu malam ('Saturday at night'), perhaps rather illogically, is equivalent to the English 'Saturday evening'.

Adverbials of time may also be clauses. The conjunctions which commonly introduce clauses which function as adverbials of time are noted in the list of conjunctions (Section 3.6.2.1).

3.7.2 Adverbials of Place

Adverbials of place answer the questions dimana? 'where?', kemana? 'where to?', and dari mana? 'where from?'.

There are no adverbials of place which are simple forms; all of them can be interpreted as consisting of a preposition followed by a noun.

The prepositions which occur are:

di-	'at, in, on'
ke-	'to'
dari	'away from'
sampai	'as far as'

They occur in the interrogatives

dimana?	'where?'

kemana?	'where to?'
dari mana?	'where from?'

They also occur in the demonstrative forms.

disini	'here'
disitu	'there'
disana	'over there, yonder'
kesini	'here (hither)'
kesitu	'there (thither)'
kesana	'over there, to a place over yonder'
dari sini	'from here (hence)'
dari situ	'from there (thence)'
dari sana	'from over there, from yonder'

They are frequently combined with locational nouns to make complex prepositions (Section 3.6.1.2).

3.7.3 Adverbials of Manner

Adverbials of manner answer the question Bagaimana? 'How?'.

They include begini 'in this manner' and begitu 'in that manner'.

A few adverbs of manner have the same form as adjectives, and only their position in the sentence structure indicates that they are adverbs and not adjectives.

Dia berkerdja keras.	'He works hard.'

Adverbials of manner which have the same form as adjectives must be directly associated with the verb, occurring either immediately before or immediately after it. The verb is usually intransitive.

Certain adverbials of manner are formed by the reduplication of other forms, particularly verbs, but occasionally adjectives or nouns.

hati-hati	'carefully'
tiba-tiba	'suddenly'
pelahan-pelahan	'slowly'

Other adverbials of manner consist of fixed concatenations of words. These are not particularly common.

sama sekali	'entirely'

Adverbs of manner are also occasionally formed from adjectives by means of the prefix *se*- and the enclitic -*nja*.

sepenuhnja	'fully'
selamanja	'eternally'

The most frequently occurring structure is, however, the preposition *dengan* (occasionally also *setjara*) followed by a nominalized adjective; the nominalization of the adjective is evidenced only by its occurrence as the object of a preposition, that is, by its occurrence in a position normally reserved for a nominal construct.

dengan tjepat	'quickly, with speed'
dengan senang	'happily, with joy'
dengan djelas	'clearly'
setjara djelas	'clearly'

In addition, adverbials of manner are formed by the preposition *dengan* occurring with nouns. The preposition *setjara* also occurs, and the two prepositions are more or less interchangeable. However, *setjara* occurs oftener with unmodified nouns while *dengan* occurs oftener with modified nouns.

setjara djantan	'valiantly'
setjara ksatriya	'heroically'
setjara sepihak	'one-sidedly'
dengan kemauan besar	'with great willingness'
dengan suara bulat	'unanimously'
dengan penuh perhatian	'with full attention'

(The object of the adjective _penuh_ and the noun _perhatian_ in the last example is an isolated anomaly, very few other examples of which are to be found.)

To denote that an action is accomplished one step or one unit at a time, a structure occurs which consists of the noun representing that unit prefixed by _se_-, 'one', followed by the word _demi_ and then the noun repeated again with the prefix.

sedikit demi sedikit	'little by little'
setapak demi setapak	'step by step'
seorang demi seorang	'person by person'

A preposition (_dengan_ or _setjara_) may also occur.

tidak dapat mentjapainja dengan sekaligus, melainkan setjara setahap-demi-setahap, setingkat-demi-setingkat.
'not able to accomplish it all at once, but stage by stage, level by level.'

Probably the form _satu persatu_ 'one by one' should be included here. This particular construction is not common with any numbers but _satu_, although it would undoubtedly be comprehensible if it did occur.

To denote that an action is carried out in an extreme degree, a structure occurs in which the prefix _se_- is added to the reduplicated form of an adjective, and this is also followed by the enclitic -_nja_.

selekas-lekasnja	'as quickly as possible'
sehormat-hormatnja	'with all possible honor'

3.7.4 Adverbials of Instrument

Closely related to the adverbials of manner are the adverbials of instrument. These are composed of the preposition dengan plus a non-personal noun.

Tutuplah pintu dengan kuntji.
'Lock the door with a key.'

Whereas the preposition dengan in adverbials of manner alternates with the preposition setjara, the preposition dengan in adverbials of instrument alternates with pakai.

Tutuplah pintu pakai kuntji.
'Lock the door with a key.'

Adverbials of instrument answer the question bagaimana? 'how?' or the more specific questions dengan apa? 'with what?', or pakai apa? 'using what?'

3.7.5 Adverbials of Accompaniment

And closely related in form to the adverbials of instrument are the adverbials of accompaniment. These are composed of the preposition dengan plus a personal noun or, less frequently, a non-personal noun.

Saja pergi kepasar dengan Ali.
'I go to the market with Ali.'

The preposition dengan in adverbials of accompaniment alternates with the prepositions sama, bersama or bersama dengan.

Saja pergi kepasar sama Ali.
'I go to the market with Ali.'

Adverbials of accompaniment answer the question dengan siapa? 'with whom?' or sama siapa? 'with whom?'.

3.7.6 Adverbials of Purpose

Adverbials of purpose answer questions which are introduced by one of these prepositions governing an interrogative word.

buat apa?	'for what purpose?'
guna siapa?	'for whose use?'

Adverbials of purpose are either prepositional phrases or clauses. Certain of the prepositions govern verb forms which are thereby nominalized. These nominalized verb forms continue to govern the sequence normal to the verb, however. Certain of the prepositions which govern verb forms also serve as conjunctions which govern sentence structures. The difference is that the verb form governed by the preposition is never accompanied by a subject, while the verb in the sentence structure governed by a conjunction usually is accompanied by a subject. This difference is, however, sufficiently subtle that it underlines the fact that prepositions and conjunctions in Indonesian are functionally very similar to each other.

Adverbials of purpose may be introduced by the prepositions bagi and guna. These prepositions govern nominal structures exclusively. They may also be introduced by the prepositions buat and untuk. These prepositions govern either nominal structures or nominalized verbs. They can further be introduced by conjunctions agar, supaja, agar supaja.

harus mendjadi tjermin buat Saudara-saudara.
'must become an example for you.'

Negara Indonesia bukan satu negara untuk satu orang.
'The Indonesian State is not one state for one man.'

Front Nasional nanti diadakan untuk menggalang seluruh tenaga daripada seluruh Rakjat.
'The National Front was later brought into being in order to activate the whole power of the whole people.'

Partai jang pada hakekatnja alat untuk menjusun pendapat umum setjara teratur, agar supaja rakjat beladjar merasai tanggung djawabnja sebagai pemangku negara dan anggota masjarakat,--
'The party which is really an instrument for forming the general opinion in an orderly manner, so that the people learns to perceive its responsibility as a directing force in the state and as a component of the community,--'

3.7.7 Adverbials of Cause

Adverbials of cause answer the questions <u>mengapa</u>? 'why?', <u>kenapa</u>? 'why?', <u>karena apa</u>? 'for what reason?', and <u>sebab apa</u>? 'for what reason?'. Of these, <u>kenapa</u>? is the least formal.

Adverbials of cause are prepositional phrases introduced by the prepositions <u>karena</u> and <u>sebab</u>, or by the conjunctions <u>karena</u> and <u>sebab</u>.

Demokrasi bisa tertindas sementera karena kesalahannja sendiri.
'Democracy can be suppressed for a while because of its own blunders.'

Tuhan memberkati kemerdekaan Indonesia, karena rakjat Indonesia memperdjuangkannja sungguh-sungguh dengan kurban jang tidak sedikit.
'God will bless the independence of Indonesia, because the people of Indonesia have striven for it intently and at no small sacrifice.'

S Y N T A X

4.0 Sentences

Form classes and their expansions combine to make sentences.

Indonesian sentences are of different types. Each type is composed of a particular selection of form-class items or their expansions. These form-class items occur most frequently in one fixed order which can therefore be considered to be the standard non-affective order; certain variations from the standard order occur; these are affective in that they provide emphasis, emotional overtones or stylistic variation. Each sentence type will be discussed first in terms of its selection of items and its standard order. Variant orders will then be noted as necessary.

The different types of sentences are interrelated in such a way that the description of one particular type is an excellent point of departure for the description of the others. This type can be considered to be basic. The first step must therefore be the isolation of this basic sentence type.

4.1 Types of Sentences

All sentences can be accomodated into three sets of binary classifications. These three classifications intersect each other. First, any sentence is either a simple or a complex sentence

(Section 4.1.1). Second, any sentence is either a subject-predicate sentence or a topic-comment sentence (Section 4.1.2). Third, any sentence is either a stimulus or a response sentence (Section 4.1.3.).

4.1.1 Simple and Complex Sentences

A simple sentence is one which has no subordinate clauses. A complex sentence is one which has one or more subordinate clauses.

Since subordinate clauses consist of a conjunction followed by a sentence structure, an ultimate analysis of all of these clauses will arrive at a string of simple sentences joined by conjunctions. Complex sentences can thus be described in terms of simple sentences.

The basic sentence is a simple sentence, then, rather than a complex sentence.

4.1.2 Subject-Predicate and Topic-Comment Sentences

A subject-predicate sentence consists, as its name implies, of a subject and a predicate. A topic-comment sentence consists of a topic and a comment; the comment has the form of a subject-predicate sentence, the topic precedes the comment and is linked to it by a simple syntactic device.

Therefore, topic-comment sentences are best described in terms of subject-predicate sentences.

The basic sentence type is, accordingly, a subject-predicate type rather than a topic-comment type.

4.1.3 Stimulus Sentences and Response Sentences

A stimulus sentence is one which is

syntactically independent of any previous sentence. The first sentence of any conversation or piece of writing is almost necessarily a stimulus sentence, and stimulus sentences may also occur subsequently in connected discourse. A response sentence, on the other hand, depends on preceding sentences for segments of its structure; these segments are not present in the response sentence, being omitted usually to avoid repetitions, but can be inferred from the preceding sentence or from the overall situation.

Response sentences do not utilize any selection of items or any order which is not to be found in a stimulus sentence; they differ from the stimulus sentence only in that they do not utilize all of the possibilities of the stimulus sentence.

Consequently, a description of the stimulus sentence will cover all aspects of the response sentence as well.

The basic sentence is a stimulus sentence rather than a response sentence.

4.1.4 The Basic Sentence

The basic sentence, then, is a simple stimulus sentence of the subject-predicate type.

(It must be noted, however, that in formal written Indonesian there are relatively few simple sentences. Reducing a complex sentence to a simple sentence by omitting the subordinate clauses or otherwise simplifying it will often produce an improbable or meaningless residue. In quoting examples, therefore, complex sentences will be used as necessary; attention will be directed to the underlying simple structure by enclosing the less germane material in parentheses in the Indonesian example only, but not in the English translation.)

4.1.5 The Modes

All Indonesian sentences occur in one of four modes: declarative (Section 4.2), interrogative (Section 4.3), imperative (Section 4.4), and exclamatory (Section 4.5). Again, a description of the declarative mode provides an easy transition to the description of the interrogative and imperative modes, while the exclamatory mode, which is infrequent in occurrence, to some extent derives from the declarative mode, and to some extent requires a discussion quite distinct from that of any of the other modes.

4.1.6 Active and Passive Voice

The predicates of Indonesian sentences are either transitive or intransitive. Those predicates which are transitive occur in either the active or the passive voice. The passive voice forms can be derived from the active forms by simple transformations.

The transitive active sentence and its corresponding passive have approximately the same value in terms of meaning. The active sentence must specify or imply a subject which denotes the performer of the action denoted by the verb; usually the object which denotes the person or thing affected by the action is also specified. The passive sentence usually specifies a subject, which in this case denotes the person or thing affected by the action, but does not necessarily specify an agent which would denote the performer of the action. The active sentence tends, then, to stress the action in its relation to the performer, while the passive tends to stress the action in its relation to the person or thing affected by it.

The order chosen here for discussing these predicates is intransitive sentences (Section 4.2.1), transitive active (Section 4.2.2) and transitive passive (Section 4.2.3).

4.2 Declarative Mode

This discussion of the Indonesian sentence begins then with a discussion of the basic sentence in the declarative mode.

4.2.1 Intransitive Predicate

The basic sentence, declarative and with an intransitive predicate, consists of a subject and a predicate, in that order. Adverbials may or may not occur; when adverbials occur, they most frequently follow the predicate. Adverbials may also precede the subject, especially if they are emphasized, or if their occurrence at the beginning of the sentence helps smooth the transition from the preceding sentence. Adverbials also occur between the subject and the predicate; usually such adverbs are single words or short prepositional phrases; clauses are rare in this position. Of course, structural material of many kinds can be introduced parenthetically (set off by commas, dashes or parentheses in writing, and by features of pause and intonation in speech); the cases considered here are those where the adverbials are integrated into the sentence structure.

The subject of this, or any, type of sentence is a nominal construct, that is, a noun or a noun-head construct, a pronoun or a pronoun-head construct, or a nominalization of some other structure.

Intransitive predicates are those which have no corresponding passive forms. Such a predicate may be a nominal, a prepositional construct, or a predicative, either an adjective or any intransitive verb, including a compound verb, either closely or loosely bound.

4.2.1.1 The predicate may be a nominal construct of any type. Sentences with this type of predicate are sometimes called equational sentences.

A nominal predicate does not ordinarily occur with the premodifiers and auxiliaries which occur with predicatives. Instead, the predicative mendjadi is introduced, thus converting the predicate from a nominal structure to a predicative with a nominal structure as dependency. The premodifiers and auxiliaries then modify the predicative. Nominal predicates are premodified, however, in rare examples.

Negara Indonesia jang kita dirikan haruslah negara gotong-rojong.
'The Indonesian state which we are building must be a "mutual-aid" state.'

An equational sentence in which the subject is an unmodified noun is rare; such a construct may be ambiguous, in that it is formally the same as a nominal construct in which the noun head is postmodified by another noun. Thus, such a collocation as

Dokter wanita

could theoretically be interpreted in two ways:

'The doctor is a woman.'
'The woman doctor.'

In speech, features of intonation and pause can make it clear which of the two structures is being used. In writing, however, the second interpretation is much more likely to be accepted. If the first interpretation is intended, the ambiguity is resolved by postmodifying the first noun (most usually with itu), so as to make only the second interpretation possible. Thus, in writing,

'The doctor is a woman.'

would almost certainly be rendered as

Dokter itu wanita.

But the use of <u>itu</u> or <u>-nja</u> to mark the end of the subject also has the effect of making the subject particular or definite, much as the use of the definite article 'the' does in English.

Sri gadis jang amat biasa.
'Sri was a completely ordinary girl.'

Si anu itu anak si anu jang kawin dengan adik si anu.
'So-and-so was the child of So-and-so who married the younger sister of So-and-so.'

Hari ini hari gadjian.
'Today is payday.'

Kera itu pada umumnja binatang (jang tidak boleh dipertjajai).
'The monkey in general is an animal which cannot be trusted.'

If the subject or the predicate of an equational sentence, or both, should happen to be structurally complex, it becomes stylistically advisable to mark the point of transition from subject to predicate more clearly.

But whether the subject is general or particular, and whether the sentence is structurally complex or not, a means of marking the transition from subject to predicate is usually employed in written Indonesian.

If the sentence is negative, the negative modifier <u>bukan</u> (with or without the predicate marker <u>-lah</u>) marks the point of transition.

If the sentence is affirmative, the predicate marker _adalah_, or, alternatively, _ialah_ occurs between the subject and the predicate. If there are other predicate markers or premodifiers (though these are rarer when the predicate is a nominal construct) _adalah_ or _ialah_ will precede all of these.

Both _adalah_ and _ialah_ appear to be morphologically complex, consisting of, respectively, the verb _ada_ and the pronoun _ia_ each followed by the enclitic -_lah_. Some justification for this point of view may be discovered in the fact that when either of these forms occurs, no other form in the predicate has the enclitic -_lah_. On the other hand, the analysis of these forms as being morphologically complex will only complicate very considerably both the discussion of the verb _ada_ and the discussion of the topic-comment sentences. For this reason, the point of view taken here is that _adalah_ and _ialah_ are syntactic units which serve as markers of the predicate structure in equational sentences, and no attempt is made to analyse them further.

Saja bukan ahli berbitjara.
'I am not an expert in speaking.'

Lahirnja idee dwitunggal diwaktu itu bukanlah suatu hal jang dibuat-buat, melainkan suatu kenjataan jang dikehendaki oleh keadaan.
'The birth of the idea of a duumvirate at that time was not a device that was patched together, but a reality which was rendered desirable by the situation.'

Presiden ialah orang Indonesia asli.
'The president shall be a native Indonesian.'

Semangat demokrasi Indonesia ialah demokrasi sosial dan kolektif.
'The soul of Indonesian democracy is a social and collective democracy.'

Apa jang terdjadi sekarang ialah KRISIS dari pada demokrasi.
'That which has developed now is a CRISIS of democracy.'

Menurut Undung-Undung Dasar '45 itu Presiden Republik Indonesia adalah kepala exekutif.
'According to the Constitution of 1945, the President of the Republic of Indonesia is an executive head of state.'

Ini adalah hukum besi dari pada sedjarah dunia!
'This is an iron law of world history!'

If, however, the predicate is a numerative, the transition from subject to predicate is not usually marked.

Rentjana jang terlantar banjak sekali.
'The programs which have been abandoned are many indeed.'

Djari kita lima setangan.
'We have five fingers on each hand.'

Banjak sekali negara-negara jang merdeka.
'Many indeed are the states which are free.'

Occasionally the predicate is in itself a complete sentence structure, usually a subordinate clause. Predicate structures, which can be construed as nominalized, also occur.

Dan akibatnja ialah bahwa Indonesia makin djauh terpisah dari tjita-tjitanja.
'And the consequence of this is that Indonesia is still farther removed from its ideal.'

Sebabnja bukanlah karena andjing air itu sedikit djumlahnja.
'The reason for this is not that the otter is few in numbers.'

Titik pertemuan mereka ialah membela demokrasi.
'Their point of consensus is the defense of democracy.'

The subject precedes the predicate in an equational sentence except in the following particular case.

As a general rule in Indonesian, when a particular structure in a sentence is to be emphasized, that structure is moved to the beginning of the sentence. When the subject of any subject-predicate sentence is to be emphasized, such a procedure is not possible, since occurrence at the beginning of the sentence is the standard unaffective position for the subject. Accordingly, when the item which is serving as the subject is to be emphasized, the subject is made the predicate of an equational sentence and this predicate is moved to the beginning of the sentence; its predicate function is marked by the enclitic -lah, since it is not in the standard position for a predicate. Then the predicate of the original unemphatic sentence is made the subject of the emphatic sentence, and, since all subjects are all nominal constructs, the predicate, if it is not already a nominal construct, must be nominalized; this is achieved by preposing jang.

Saja seorang guru.
'I am a teacher.'

Sajalah seorang guru.
'It is I who am a teacher.'

Saja pergi.
'I went.'

Sajalah jang pergi.
'It was I who went.'

Lemak itulah jang menjebabkan maka air tidak melekat.

'It is this grease which causes the water not to stick.'

Pemerintah itulah jang stabil sampai pada pemulihan kedaulatan pada achir tahun 1949 oleh Nederland.
'It was that government which was stable until the restoration of sovereignty at the end of 1949 by the Netherlands.'

Menurut djalan pikiran ini, diantara badan-badan jang kerdjasama dalam melakukan pemerintahan, Parlemen dan Pemerintah, Parlemenlah jang terkuat.
'According to this line of thought, between the bodies which work together in the conducting of the government, the Parliament and the Government, it is the Parliament which is stronger.'

Inilah jang mendjadi minimum-eis.
'It was this that became a minimum for them.'

Djustru inilah prinsip saja jang kedua.
'It is precisely this which is my second principle.'

4.2.1.2 The predicate may be a prepositional construct. The subject precedes the predicate. Sentences of this type are not particularly common in formal Indonesian, but are frequent in spoken Indonesian.

Satu buat semua, semua buat satu
'All for one, and one for all'

Kedaulatan adalah ditangan rakjat.
'The decision is in the hands of the people.'

Hanja satu jang sulit untuk mentjari kontak ialah dengan AU.
'The only one which was difficult to contact was with the Air Force.'

Tetapi memburu mangsa untuk dimakannja sendiri tidaklah lagi dilakukannja.
'But to kill prey to be eaten by it itself is no longer in its pattern of behavior.'

On occasion, the predicate precedes the subject.

Seperti manusia tabiatnja dalam mengasuh anaknja itu.
'Its behavior in taking care of its young is like (that of) man.'

4.2.1.3 The predicate may be a predicative. Those predicatives which govern a dependency will ordinarily do so, and the predicate consists of both predicative and dependency. Sentences which have as a predicate either an adjectival predicative, or any verbal predicative which was described in Section 3.2.3 as intransitive, copulative, amphoteric without an object, or as governing a predicative structure, are intransitive sentences of this type.

Sentences which consist of a subject and a predicate which does not contain a dependency, have the standard order subject, predicate. The inverse order also occurs on occasion, especially when the predicate is to be given special emphasis; in such a case the predicate is commonly marked by the enclitic -<u>lah</u>, or by predicate modifiers which establish its function.

Rumah itu besar.	'That house is large.'
Besar rumah itu.	'That house is <u>large</u>.'
Besarlah rumah itu.	'That house is <u>large</u>.'

Siti pulang.	'Siti went home.'
Pulang Siti.	'Siti <u>went home</u>.'
Pulanglah Siti.	'Siti <u>went home</u>.'

Petisi itu tidak berhasil.
'This petition was unsuccessful.'

Banjak tikus mati.
'Many rats die.'

Kelandjutannja, korupsi dan demoralisasi meradjalela.
'As a consequence, corruption and demoralization reigned.'

Ia bersidang sedikit-dikitnja sekali lima tahun.
'It has been meeting more or less for five years in a row.'

Ini semua terdjadi tanpa dengan mempergunakan kekerasan.
'All of this took place without the use of force.'

Presiden dan Wakil Presiden bersumpah menurut agama,... sebagai berikut:
'The President and the Vice-President shall take an oath, in accordance with their religion,... as follows:

Rusa betina tidak berangga.
'The female deer has no antlers.'

Sang klerk dengan satu medja, empat kursi, satu zitje, satu tempat tidur: kawin.
'The worthy clerk who has one table, four chairs, a settee and a bed, gets married.'

Keributan dan keramaian siang seolah-olah berhenti.
'The bustle and commotion of the day, so to speak, stop.'

Dengan matanja jang bulat tikus itu dapat djuga melihat.
'With those round eyes of his the rat can really see.'

Tetapi sesudah itu semangat ultra-demokratis muntjul kembali.
'But after this the ultra-democratic sentiment

arose again.'

In the following examples, the predicate precedes the subject. The predicate is not marked by -lah.

Disebelah demokrasi politik harus pula berlaku demokrasi ekonomi.
'Alongside of the political democracy there must also exist economic democracy.'

Achirnja terdapat 19 buah.
'Finally there got to be nineteen.'

Kadang-kadang terdengar bunji (seakan-akan luak mengedjar tikus).
'From time to time can be heard a sound as if a civet cat is chasing a mouse.'

Oleh karena itu sungguh menggembirakan sekali maksud penerbit.
'For this reason, the intention of the publisher is really most gratifying.'

Akan tetapi lenjap dia tidak.
'But disappear it will not.'

Here also the predicate precedes the subject but is marked by -lah, which is enclitic to the first item of the predicate structure.

Begitulah terdjadi wabah pes.
'Thus begins an epidemic of the plague.'

Maka timbullah krisis kabinet.
'And then there arose a cabinet crisis.'

Maka terdjadilah peristiwa jang disebut tadi pada permulaan karangan ini.
'Then occurred that event which was mentioned earlier at the beginning of this article.'

(Apabila tanduk itu patah,) maka keluarlah darah.
'When this horn is broken, blood comes out.'

Didalam 1933 barulah datang saatnja jang beliau dapat merebut kekuasaan.
'Only in 1933 did the hour come when he was able to seize power.'

(Maka saja berkata, baru djikalau dimikian, baru djikalau dimikian,) hiduplah Islam Indonesia, (dan bukan Islam jang hanja diatas bibir sadja).
'And so I say, if it is indeed thus, if it is indeed thus, the Islam of Indonesia is alive, and is not an Islam which exists only upon the lips.'

Tidaklah mengherankan, bahwa musuh-musuhnja mempergunakan segala tipu-muslihat akan mendekati dia dengan tiada membangkitkan suara sama sekali.
'It is not surprising that its enemies use every trick and stratagem in order to get near it without making any sound at all.'

As in the case of equational sentences, a sentence in which the predicate is an adjective and the subject is a simple noun will be ambiguous in that it will have the same form as a nominal construct in which the head noun is modified by an adjective.

Rumah besar	'The house is big.' 'The big house'

The ambiguity is resolved by postmodifying the subject, usually with the determiner itu, if no other postmodifier occurs.

Rumah itu besar.	'The house is big.'

In structurally more complicated sentences or in more formal style, adalah or ialah may also occur to mark the juncture between the subject and the predicate.

Keislaman saja djauh belum sempurna.
'My Mohammedanism is as yet far from perfect.'

Tetapi pendapat sematjam itu tidak benar.
'But an opinion such as that is not correct.'

Sajang djumlahnja makin lama makin berkurang.
'Unfortunately its numbers get smaller as time goes by.'

Indonesia jang adil jang ditunggu-tunggu masih djauh sadja.
'The Indonesia of Justice which has been waited for and waited for is still far away.'

Penghargaan manusia terhadap kepada kera itu tiadalah sama.
'The value men see in monkeys is not uniform.'

When the adjective predicate precedes the subject, there is not the same potential for ambiguity and the predicate need not be marked, though it most frequently is.

Lain halnja (kalau ada kamu dengar riuh-rendah dikandang ajam).
'The situation is different if it happens that you hear an uproar in the chicken run.'

Karena itu bodohlah kita, kalau...
'For this reason we would be stupid if...'

Demikianlah saja punja djawab atas pertanjaan Paduka Tuan Ketua.
'Such is my answer to the question of the honorable chairman.'

Dalam waktu satu malam sadja habislah buah sekebun itu.
'In the period of only one night the fruit of that whole orchard is gone.'

Dan mulai saat itu tamatlah pada hakekatnja sedjarah dwitunggal dalam politik Indonesia.
'And from that moment the history of the duumvirate in the politics of Indonesia was in truth finished.'

Usually, when the predicate is an adjective, and the subject is in itself a subordinate sentence structure or a nominalized predicative, the predicate-subject order occurs, but not invariably.

Bahwa kalong itu binatang jang merugikan sudahlah terang.
'That the flying fox is an animal which does damage is already clear.'

Untung benar bagi kita bahwa kampret itu memakan serangga.
'It is fortunate for us that the bat eats insects.'

Tetapi diantara Masjumi dan dua lain itu sukar mentjapai persesuaian paham.
'But between the Masjumi party and the two others it is difficult to reach a consensus of opinion.'

Memang tak mudah membangun suatu demokrasi di Indonesia jang lantjar djalannja.
'Certainly it is not easy to build a democracy in Indonesia whose operation will be smooth.'

Intransitive sentences which consist of a subject and a predicate which does contain a dependency, have the standard order: subject, predicative, dependency. Adverbials do not occur between the predicative and its dependency unless the dependency is not closely bound.

(Compound predicatives, such as bertanam padi, 'to make a living by raising rice', are inseparable, and padi is an integral part of the predicate, and not a dependency at all.)

Predicatives with closely bound dependencies, such as the unique and invariable stereotype naik hadji, 'to go on the pilgrimage to Mecca', are inseparable and no adverbial intervenes between naik and hadji.

Predicatives with loosely bound dependencies, such as naik sepeda, 'to go by bicycle' (where, at least in theory, there is a variety of forms which can be substituted for sepeda, such as mobil 'car', kereta api 'train', kapal terbang 'airplane' and so on, and where sepeda can theoretically be modified in various ways, such as naik sepeda kakak), may have adverbial material occurring between predicative and dependency, but this is uncommon.

Ali naik hadji.	'Ali went to Mecca.'
Ali naik sepeda.	'Ali goes by bicycle.'

Patut ia pandai benar berlari.
'Accordingly it is very clever at running.'

Pertjektjokan politik dipusat besar pengaruhnja kebawah.
'The political squabbling in the center was great in its influence toward decline.'

Gigi depannja (gigi pengiris) lebih tadjam dari pada gigi manusia.
'Its front teeth (gnawing teeth) are sharper than the teeth of man.'

Sebab itu pula sistim jang dilahirkan Soekarno itu tidak akan lebih pandjang umurnja dari Soekarno sendiri.
'For this reason again, the system which has been brought into existence by Sukarno will not be longer-lived than Sukarno himself.'

Madjelis Permusjawaratan Rakjat terdiri atas tiga golongan utusan rakjat.
'The People's Consultative Council consists of

three groups of delegates of the people.'

Dalam merealisasinja orang lupa akan rangkaiannja dengan persamaan dan persaudaraan.
'In achieving that, people forgot about its connection with equality and fraternity.'

Luak gemar djuga memakan buah-buahan jang lunak dan manis.
'The civet cat also likes to eat various kinds of soft, sweet fruit.'

Lebih dari separoh berasal dari pegawai negeri jang dalam zaman Hindia Belanda tidak mempunjai pengalaman politik.
'More than half hailed from the government workers who, in the period of the Dutch East Indies, did not have any political experience.'

Other orders are possible. Where both the dependency and the subject are nominals, and the dependency is not postmodified, there must be, in speech, an appreciable pause between the dependency and the subject if they occur in that order; otherwise the subject may be construed as modifying the dependency. The occurrence of the enclitic -lah on the dependency avoids any ambiguity.

Naik hadji Ali.	'Ali has gone to Mecca.' 'It's gone to Mecca, Ali is.'
(Naik sepeda Ali.) Naik sepedalah Ali. (Sepeda Ali naik.) Sepedalah Ali naik.)	'Ali goes by bicycle.'

On the whole, however, any order but the standard order is extremely uncommon in written Indonesian.

The following sentence is in the order: dependency, subject, predicative, with the enclitic -pun postposed to the dependency and the premodifier sangat preposed to the predicative.

Melompat dan menarik dirinja keatas pun ia sangat pandai.
'At leaping and also at pulling itself up it is extremely clever.'

Here the order is predicative, subject, dependency:

Berani dia menjerang ular berbisa.
'It is brave enough to attack poisonous snakes.'

4.2.2 Transitive Predicate Active

Transitive sentences are those which have corresponding passive forms.

The basic sentence, declarative and with a transitive active predicate, can be subdivided into three groups. There are those in which the predicative (which is always a verb) governs one object, those in which it governs two objects, and those in which it governs an object and an object complement.

4.2.2.1 The singly transitive sentence has a subject and a predicate which consists of a verb governing one object; it occurs in the standard order: subject, verb, object. Adverbials may occur after the object, before the subject, between the subject and the verb and, more rarely, between the verb and its object.

Mala melihat burung itu.
'Mala sees the bird.'

Ia memilih Presiden dan Wakil Presiden.
'It chooses the President and the Vice-President.'

Tuhan memberkati kemerdekaan Indonesia.
'God has laid his blessing on the independence

of Indonesia.'

Marx dan Engels menerima Darwin.
'Marx and Engels accepted Darwin.'

Stalin mengenal sekali Lenin.
'Stalin knew Lenin well.'

Dan orang tjoba membuat konsepsi demokrasi Indonesia jang moderen, berdasarkan demokrasi desa jang asli itu.
'And people try to build the concept of a modern democracy, based on the native village democracy.'

Analisa sosial menundjukkan, bahwa demokrasi asli Indonesia kuat bertahan dibawah feodalisme.
'Sociological analysis shows that the native democracy of Indonesia was strongly entrenched in the feudal period.'

Demokrasi politik sadja tidak dapat melaksanakan persamaan dan persaudaraan.
'Political democracy alone can not generate equality and fraternity.'

Sedjarah Indonesia sedjak 10 tahun jang achir ini banjak memperlihatkan pertentangan antara idealisme dan realita.
'The history of Indonesia during these last ten years demonstrates clearly the struggle between idealism and reality.'

Jang Kristen menjembah Tuhan menurut petundjuk Isa al Masih,
'The Christian worships God according to the teachings of Jesus the Messiah,'

Kita bukan sadja harus mendirikan negara Indonesia Merdeka, (tetapi kita harus menudju pula kepada kekeluargaan bangsa-bangsa).
'We must not only establish a Free Indonesia, but we must take our place once more within the family of nations.'

Badjing membuat sarang dipuntjak pohon, biasanja dipohon kelapa.
'The squirrel makes its nest in the top of a tree, usually in a coconut tree.'

Ikan jang tidak sehat menurunkan ikan jang tidak sehat pula.
'Unhealthy fish beget more unhealthy fish.'

Alam selalu mendjaga keseimbangan diri.
'Nature always preserves her own balance.'

As has been pointed out, an adverbial may precede the subject. On occasion this adverbial may be marked by the enclitic -lah postposed to its last member so that the division between the adverbial and the subject is clearly marked. The presence of -lah is not obligatory; it occurs more frequently with adverbials which would otherwise terminate with the determiner itu; otherwise itu could be construed either as postmodifying a nominal construct in the adverbial, or as the subject following the adverbial. In some cases the connective maka may occur before the subject, either instead of -lah at the end of the adverbial, or along with it.

Sebelumnja saja minta maaf.
'First of all, I beg pardon.'

Hati-hati kita mendekati kera!
'We approach a monkey with great caution!'

Umumnja orang menjangka, bahwa segala binatang-berburu itu ialah binatang jang mendatangkan kerugian belaka.
'Generally people think that all these predatory animals are animals which do nothing but cause damage.'

Pada siang hari tjahaja matahari terlalu menjilaukan matanja.
'In the middle of the day the brilliance of the

sun dazzles its eyes too much.'

Sekali beranak rusa betina melahirkan dua ekor anak.
'When she gives birth, the female deer bears two fawns.'

Diluar dari itu kita tidak mengalami nationale staat.
'Outside of this we have not established a national state.'

Sebab itu ia sering mentjapai jang sebaliknja dari jang ditudjunja.
'For this reason he frequently achieves the opposite of what he intends.'

Patutlah orang Islam memandang dia sebagai binatang jang nadjis.
'Moslems rightly consider it to be an unclean animal.' (or, if patutlah is construed as the predicate, and the balance of the sentence as a sentence structure nominalized by the position in which it occurs, namely, the subject position) 'It is right that Moslems consider it to be an unclean animal.'

Dan diatas kelima dasar itulah kita mendirikan Negara Indonesia
'And on those five principles we shall build the Indonesian state'

Didalam masa peperangan itulah kita mendirikan negara Indonesia.
'In that time of war we built the Indonesian nation.'

Didalam Indonesia Merdeka itulah kita memerdekakan rakjat kita.
'Within that free Indonesia we will liberate our people.'

Oleh karna itulah maka tahun 1959 menduduki tempat jang istimewa dalam sedjarah Perdjoangan Nasional kita, satu tempat jang unik!
'For this reason the year 1959 occupies a special place in the history of our National Struggle, a place which is unique!'

Apabila tikus itu mati dan dikelilingnja itu tak ada tikus lain, barulah kutu itu mentjari manusia.
'When this rat dies, and in its vicinity there is no other rat, then the flea will seek out a human being.'

In some cases, where the verb structure includes a premodifier or an auxiliary, the premodifier or auxiliary occurs before the subject, and the remainder of the verb structure occurs after the subject; this is a stylistic device, more favored by some authors than by others.

Pada hemat kami dapat djuga guru memilih beberapa peladjaran sadja dengan tiada menguruangi atau mengabaikan maksud susunan buku ini.
'In our opinion the teacher will also be able to choose a certain number of lessons only without diminishing or avoiding the purpose of the arrangement of this book.'

Sebab itu perlu mereka meluangkan tempat dalam kekuasaan politik bagi pemimpin-pemimpin jang lain itu.
'For this reason they must create a place in the political power structure for those other delegates.'

Hampir tak dapat kita mengikuti terbang kampret itu dengan mata.
'We almost can not follow the flight of the bat with our eyes.'

Begitu dapatlah ia sekaligus menangkap dua-tiga ekor ketam.

'In this way it is able to seize two or three crabs at the same time.'

Other orders are also possible for stylistic effect and emphasis. The only orders which merit consideration, however, are verb, object, subject, or object, subject, verb. Unless the termination of the object structure is clearly marked (by pause in speech, by itu or some other marker in writing) the object-subject sequence may be construed as nominal post-modified by nominal, and ambiguity will arise.

These orders occur on occasion in speech, but are extremely rare in written Indonesian.

Melihat burung itu Mala. 'Mala does see the bird.'
Burung itu Mala melihat. 'Mala sees the bird.'

4.2.2.2 The doubly transitive sentence has a subject and a predicate which consists of a verb governing two objects (the primary object and the secondary object); it occurs in the standard order: subject, verb, secondary object, primary object.

Dia membelikan saja sebuah buku.
'He bought me a book.'

Unless the secondary object follows the verb immediately, it is replaced by a prepositional construction employing either the preposition untuk or kepada followed by the noun construct which serves as the secondary object.

Dia membelikan sebuah buku untuk saja.
'He bought me a book.'

Dia mendjualkan saja sepeda itu.
'He sold the bicycle for me.'

Dia membawakan temannja surat itu.
'He brought his friend the letter.'

Kami mentjarikan dia suatu pekerdjaan.
'We looked for a job for him.'

Ajah mengirimi anaknja lima rupiah.
'The father sent his son five rupiahs.'

This prepositional phrase has the freedom of occurrence of an adverb. The remaining three components of the sentence, the subject, the verb, and the primary object, then occur in those combinations which are possible in transitive sentences with one object. In such a case, if the verb has a suffix whose primary function is to classify it as a doubly transitive verb, the suffix may no longer occur, if the prepositional phrase replacing the secondary object is too far dissociated from the verb.

Doubly transitive sentences are uncommon in written Indonesian and, in the active voice, uncommon in conversational material in novels and stories. The secondary object is regularly marked by a preposition in a more formal style.

4.2.2.3 The transitive-copulative sentence has a subject and a predicate which consists of a verb governing an object and an object complement; it occurs in the standard order: subject, verb, object, object complement. The object complement is a nominal structure or a predicative structure.

Dia mengira saja orang djahat.
'He thought me a malicious person.'

Dia mengira dirinja pembangun revolusi.
'He thinks of himself as the revolution builder.'

Kami menjangka dia orang Palembang.
'We thought he was a Palembang man.'

Mereka menjanggap saja jang tersenior.
'They considered me to be the senior officer.'

Pemerintah menganggap perkembangan itu perkembangan progresif.
'The government considers the development a progressive one.'

Istrinja mengira suaminja takut.
'His wife thinks that her husband is afraid.'

Stalin menjangka kekuatannja terletak dalam mamuaskan segala matjam hasrat-hasrat manusia.
'Stalin considered his power was based on satisfying all kinds of desires of humanity.'

Kita melihat kutjing duduk berpanas-panas dimuka pintu.
'We see the cat sitting sunning itself in front of the door.'

On occasion, a premodifier of the verb precedes the subject.

Perlu orang-orangnja merasa diri bersatu.
'The people must feel themselves united.'

Non-standard orders are uncommon, especially in written material.

Occasionally, it may happen that the entire predicate, consisting of verb, direct object and object complement, precedes the subject.

Mengira saja orang djahat dia.
'Thought I was malicious, he did.'

With certain verbs, the object-complement may occur alternatively as a prepositional structure (the preposition is usually <u>sebagai</u> 'as'), and this prepositional structure functions adverbially; the sentence is then a singly transitive sentence.

Golongan minoritet menganggap perbuatan Presiden itu sebagai suatu tindak-perkosa, tetapi...

'The minority group considers this action of the President as a violation, but...'

4.2.3 Transitive Predicate Passive

Any basic sentence, declarative and with a transitive active predicate, corresponds to a passive sentence which can be derived from it by a series of transformations. Some of these transformations are the same for all types of active sentence, and some require modification depending on the specific type of active sentence in question.

The description given for the sentence with the singly transitive verb is applicable in general to all types of transitive sentence with only minor modifications.

4.2.3.1 In the singly transitive sentence, the object of the active sentence becomes the subject of the passive sentence. The subject of the active sentence becomes the agent of the passive sentence. The active verb loses its prefix meN-, and this is replaced by the prefix di-, except when the order is such that the agent immediately precedes the verb head (or, perhaps, the verb structure).

The standard word order for the passive sentence is freer than that for the active sentence. Perhaps the most common order is: subject, verb, agent. In this case, the verb has the prefix di- replacing the prefix meN- of the active, and the agent may either be marked by the preposition oleh before it, or it may not be so marked. If the agent is a pronoun, the free form or the enclitic form of the pronoun may be used with the preposition oleh, and either form may likewise be used if the preposition oleh is not present; in this case, the enclitic form of the pronoun is attached to the verb. Thus the active sentence

Dia membeli buku itu. 'He bought the book.'

may be rendered in the subject-verb-agent order as

Buku itu dibeli oleh dia. 'The book was bought by
Buku itu dibeli olehnja. him.'
Buku itu dibeli dia.
Buku itu dibelinja.

(It is felt by many grammarians that the prefix _di-_ in the passive should be associated only with subjects in the third person, and never with subjects in the first or second persons. Thus, the active sentence

Saja membeli buku itu.

should not be rendered, according to these grammarians, as

Buku itu dibeli oleh saja.

because _dibeli_ is third person and _saja_ is first person. Other grammarians do not accept this stricture and freely admit sentences of the type given here. On the whole, sentences such as these are widely used by speakers of Indonesian.)

Binatang itu didjual orang.
'(These animals are sold by people.)'
'People sell these animals.'

Ketam ditangkapnja dengan kaki dan mulutnja.
'(The crabs are caught by it with its feet and its mouth.)'
'It catches the crabs with its feet and its mouth.'

Betul tidaknja belum pernah dibuktikan orang dengan njata.
'(The truth or not of this has not yet been proved by men clearly.)'
'Whether this is true or not has not yet been clearly established.'

Tupai tidak berapa dikenal orang.
'(The tupai (rat-squirrel) is not so much known by people.)'
'People are less familiar with the tupai.'

Segala pergerakan dan sembojan nasional diperalatkan mereka.
'All of the national movements and slogans are used as tools by them.'

Presiden dibantu oleh satu orang Wakil Presiden.
'The president shall be aided by one vice-president.'

Semua anggota ditundjuk oleh Presiden.
'All members are appointed by the President.'

Ini disebabkan oleh sistim pemilihan jang terlalu demokratis.
'This was caused by a system of franchise which was too democratic.'

Semuanja itu harus dihadapi oleh tentera.
'All of this had to be faced by the army.'

,djika kemerdekaan itu tidak diberkati oleh Tuhan.
',if this independence is not blessed by God.'

Akan tetapi darah manusia itu tidak berapa digemari oleh kutu tikus.
'But the blood of man is not particularly relished by the rat flea.'

Pergaulan hidup harus diliputi oleh suasana kekeluargaan dan persaudaraan.
'A lively social interchange must be enveloped by an atmosphere of family feeling and brotherhood.'

A permutation of this order, in which the items occur in the order: verb, agent, subject, has exactly the same possibilities, except that the subject occurs in final position instead of in initial position.

Dibeli oleh dia buku itu. Dibeli olehnja buku itu. Dibeli dia buku itu. Dibelinja buku itu.	'The book was bought by him.'

But again, unless the transition from a noun agent to the subject is marked (by a pause in speaking and by postmodification of the agent in writing at the very least), ambiguity will be possible.

This order, accordingly, tends to be restricted to those cases where the agent is a pronoun.

Maka ditjabutinja kaki-kaki ketam itu dan dibuangnja.
'(Then the crab's legs are torn off and thrown away by it.)'
'Then it tears off the crab's legs and throws them away.'

Another common order is: subject, agent, verb. In this case, the verb does not have the prefix meN- of the active, nor any prefix to replace it. If the verb has other prefixes, such as per-, these are retained. The agent is not marked by the preposition oleh, but becomes proclitic to the verb head, that is, it must occur immediately before the verb head. If the verb head is expanded by means of auxiliaries or predicate markers, those which precede the verb head must also precede the agent in this case. In other words, the agent is fused to the verb form, even though, in writing, there may be a space between the agent and the verb form. No other structure may intervene between agent and verb. If the agent is a pronoun and the pronoun has a proclitic form, the proclitic form may be used, and is attached directly to the passive verb form.

Though the agent may theoretically occur in any form, in practice only agents which are structurally simple are found. Pronouns are common; simple nouns are found, modified nouns are rare and a noun with complex modification simply does not occur except in contrived situations.

The following pairs of sentences correspond directly in that one is active and the other passive.

Dia membeli buku itu.	'He bought that book.'
Buku itu dia beli.	'That book was bought by him.'
Aku membeli buku itu.	'I bought that book.'
Buku itu kubeli.	'That book was bought by me.'
Ali akan membeli buku itu.	'Ali will buy that book.'
Buku itu akan Ali beli.	'That book will be bought by Ali.'

Memang tidak segala bunji dapat kita dengar.
'(Certainly not all sounds can be heard by us.)'
'We can certainly not hear all sounds.'

Itu dapat kita lihat pada matanja.
'(This can be seen by us in its eyes.)'
'We can see this in its eyes.'

"Weltanschauung" ini sudah lama harus kita bulatkan didalam hati kita.
'(This philosophical outlook should already have been developed by us in our hearts long ago.)'
'We should already have developed this philosophical outlook in our hearts long ago.'

Apa-apa jang belum memuaskan, kita bitjarakan didalam permusjawaratan.
'(Whatever does not yet satisfy will be discussed by us in our representative body.)'
'We will discuss whatever is not yet satisfactory in our representative body.'

Remdepan, tanpa aku rem, mengerem sendiri.
'(The front brake, without being braked by me, braked itself.)'
'The front brake grabbed, with no help from me.'

Sudah berapa lama andjing itu mendjadi "temam serumah" bagi manusia, tidaklah dapat kita ketahui.
'(How long ago the dog became a "houseguest" for man cannot be known to us.)'
'We cannot know how long ago the dog became man's "houseguest".'

Bagaimana kalau dia saja sekolahkan di Djakarta.
'(How about if he is sent to school by me in Djakarta?)'
'What if I send him to school in Djakarta?'

On occasion a premodifier of the verb or an auxiliary occurs before the subject.

Pada waktu sendja-malampun dapat ia kita ketahui dengan mudah.
'(At the time of twilight or even night it can be known by us easily.)'
'We can know it easily at twilight or even at night.'

The stricture that no other structure may intervene between the agent and the head of the passive verb form in this particular order is not universally observed. Such a sentence as

Buku itu Ali akan beli.

does occur, even if it is not condoned in formal Indonesian. This construction occurs with differing frequencies in different authors, and at different periods of one author's production. It seems, on the whole, that it is becoming less frequent, and more recent writings provide fewer examples than earlier writings.

Badan permusiawaratan jang kita akan buat,...
'(The representative body which will be made by us...)'
'The representative body which we are going to build...'

,dan jang kini pula kita harus dirikan bersama-sama.
'(,and which now again must be built by us together.)'
',and which we now again must build together.'

A common variation of this order is agent, verb, subject, particularly when the subject is complex, or is a subordinate clause.

Tetapi buat tahun 1959 saja akan beri sebutan lain.
'(But for the year 1959 by me will be taken another saying.)'
'But for the year 1959 I will choose another label.'

Dalam suatu kritik terhadap konsepsinja kira-kira tiga tahun jang lalu saja bandingkan dia dengan Mephistopheles dalam hikajat Goethe's Faust.
'In a criticism of his concept about three years ago I compared him (by me was compared he) with Mephistopheles in Goethe's story of Faust.'

Berpuluh-puluh tahun sudah saja pikirkan dia, ialah dasar-dasarnja Indonesia Merdeka.
'Some tens of years ago they, that is, the basic principles of a Free Indonesia, were already thought out by me.'

Tuan-tuan akan dapati tidak lain tidak bukan hati Islam.
'(By you will be found nothing more nor less than a Moslem heart.)'
'You will find nothing more nor less than a Moslem heart.'

Disinilah kita usulkan kepada pemimpin-pemimpin rakjat, apa-apa jang kita rasa perlu bagi perbaikan.
'Here then we shall propose (by us will be proposed) to the representatives of the people whatever we feel (by us is felt) necessary for improvement.'

Sekarang kami tanjakan, pernahkah kamu mengetahui bahwa Dewan Djeneral akan mengadakan coup.
'(Now by us is asked,...)'
'Now we ask, had you ever heard that the Council of Generals was going to stage a coup.'

In all other possible sentence orders, which are of less common occurrence in formal writing, the agent must be marked by the preposition oleh, and the passive verb will have the prefix di-.

Dibeli buku itu oleh dia. 'The book was bought by
Oleh dia buku itu dibeli. him.'
Oleh dia dibeli buku itu.

Since the passive form de-emphasizes the doer of the action denoted by the verb, it happens that the agent is not specified at all in many cases. The standard order is subject, verb.

Kemerdekaan individu diutamakan.
'Individual freedom is stressed.'

Pertanjaan itu boleh diubah, ditambah, dikurangi atau dilalui.
'These questions can be altered, supplemented, reduced in number or passed over.'

Sebab itu ia tidak dapat dilenjapkan untuk selama-lamanja.
'For that reason it cannot be banished forever.'

Undang-undang Dasar Negara manapun tidak dapat dimengerti, kalau hanja dibatja tekstnja sadja.
'Any constitution whatsoever cannot be understood,

if only its text is read, and nothing more.'

Daerah Indonesia akan dibagi dalam daerah propinsi.
'The territory of Indonesia will be divided into provincial areas.'

agar supaja Hari Ulang Tahun AB jang ke XX ini diperingati dengan meriah.
'in order that the twentieth anniversary of the Armed Forces be celebrated gloriously.'

Untuk tidak merugikan kepentingan umum maka pemilikan dan penguasaan tanah jang melampaui batas tidak diperkenankan.
'In order not to impair the common good, possession and control of the land which exceeds these bounds is not permitted.'

Segala Badan Negara dan Peraturan jang ada masih langsung berlaku, selama belum diadakan jang baru menurut Undang-undang Dasar itu.
'All Bodies of the State and all Regulations which are in existence shall still continue to be valid as long as a new one is not established in accordance with this Constitution.'

A common variant order is verb-subject.

Dalam Undang-undang Dasar 1950 ditetapkan sistim kabinet parlementer.
'In the Constitution of 1950 the parliamentary cabinet system was established.'

, untuk diatasnja didirikan gedung Indonesia Merdeka jang kekal dan abadi.
', in order that, upon it, there might be raised the structure of a Free Indonesia which would be lasting and eternal.'

Tidak dapat disangkal, bahwa pemimpin-pemimpin partai politik kita dalam masa 10 tahun jang achir ini gagal dalam melaksanakan tugasnja.
'It cannot be denied that the delegates of our

political parties in the period of the last ten years have failed in the execution of their duties.'

4.2.3.2 In a doubly transitive sentence, only the secondary object can become the subject of the passive sentence. The passive sentence will then have the order: subject, verb, primary object; the agent will either follow the primary object, or, less commonly, precede the subject. In each of these cases, the agent must be marked by _oleh_, and the passive verb will have the prefix _di_-. A third possibility is that the agent will follow the verb and precede the primary object; in this case the preposition _oleh_ is optional, but the verb must have the prefix _di_-. A fourth possibility is that the agent will be proclitic to the verb. In this case, the agent is not marked by the preposition _oleh_, and the verb will not have the prefix _di_-. Thus, corresponding to the doubly transitive active sentence

Dia membelikan saja buku itu.
'He bought that book for me.'

the following passive transformations are possible:

Saja dibelikan buku itu oleh dia (olehnja).
Oleh dia (olehnja) saja dibelikan buku itu.
Saja dibelikan (oleh) dia buku itu.
Saja dia belikan buku itu.

Such forms are colloquial rather than formal, however, and occur only in conversational material in written Indonesian.

Engkau akan kubelikan piano.
'(You will by me be bought a piano.)'
'I am going to buy you a piano.'

Ia diserahi pelaksanaan eksekusi.
'He was entrusted with the carrying out of the execution.'

It is to be noted that passive formations in which the primary object of the doubly transitive sentence is made the subject of a passive sentence simply do not occur. The primary object can become the subject in the passive only if the secondary object is marked by a preposition (usually untuk, buat, or kepada), and so given the function of an adverb. Thus, such a sentence as

Buku itu dibelikan oleh dia untuk saja.

or

Buku itu dikirimkan oleh dia kepada saja.

occurs, but it occurs as a singly transitive sentence, and is then capable of the various changes in word order described in the preceding section. Again, doubly transitive verbs which are distinguished from singly transitive verbs by the suffix -kan or -i may lose the suffix, particularly if it is -i, when the secondary object is adverbialized by being marked by a preposition.

4.2.3.3 The transitive-copulative active sentence is transformed into the passive in the same way as the singly transitive active sentence, except that the object complement is not usually separated from the verb head, which precedes it. The agent then has three possible positions: after the complement (oleh is necessary), before the subject (oleh again necessary), or proclitic to the verb (oleh not permitted).

Ali menjangka saja orang Palembang.
'Ali thought I was a Palembang man.'

can be transformed to the passive as

Saja disangka orang Palembang oleh Ali.
Oleh Ali saja disangka orang Palembang.
Saja Ali sangka orang Palembang.

Similarly, the sentence

Ali menganggap soal itu beres.
'Ali considered the problem settled.'

can be transformed to the passive as

Soal itu dianggap beres oleh Ali.
Oleh Ali soal itu dianggap beres.
Soal itu Ali anggap beres.

The passive forms are of commoner occurrence in formal Indonesian than the corresponding active forms.

(Sentences such as those just given can also occur as:

Ali menjangka bahwa saja orang Palembang.
Ali menganggap bahwa soal itu beres.

Such sentences are no longer to be regarded as transitive-copulative, but as simply transitive, with the nominal clause, here introduced by bahwa, as the object. The only possible passive sentences would be

Bahwa saja orang Palembang Ali sangka.
Bahwa soal itu beres Ali anggap.

Such passive sentences are not, however, of frequent occurrence.)

Saja dianggap jang tersenior.
'I was considered to have the greatest seniority.'

Oleh karena itu andjing dinamai machluk jang berdjalan djari.
'For this reason the dog is called a creature

that walks on its toes.'

Buku saja ini mungkin dianggap aneh.
'This book of mine may possibly be thought strange.'

Tak mau dikira takut.
'I didn't want to be thought to be afraid.'

Luak jang djinak biasanja diberi makan buah-buahan.
'The tame civet cat is usually given fruit to eat.'

The object-complement alternates, after certain verbs, with a prepositional structure.

Madjelis itu akan betul-betul dapat dianggap sebagai pendjelmaan rakjat.
'This council will truly be able to be considered as a personification of the people.'

4.2.4 Minor Declarative Sentences

There are a small number of minor sentence types which are best described in connection with the basic sentence.

Three types of minor sentence involve the verb _ada_ as the head of the predicate. The remaining sentence type has no subject.

4.2.4.1 In the first of these minor sentence types, the verb _ada_ is associated with a nominal construct which, in standard sentence order, follows it. It is difficult to decide whether this represents a sentence type in which there is no subject, and the verb has a single object, or whether it is a subject-predicate construction which customarily occurs in the order predicate, subject. Probably the second interpretation is the better, because the verb _ada_ is not transitive; there is no corresponding passive sentence structure. The verb _ada_ refers to the existence of the referent of the noun construct.

Selalu ada jang berkawal.
'There is always one who watches.'

dengan tidak ada ketjualinja
'without exception'

Tetapi lebih dari itu tidak ada persamaan.
'But more than this, there is no equality.'

Zhivago, sebab ditanah-milik ajah ada tjukup uang...
'Zhivago, because in his father's private property there is enough money...'

Tidak ada jang setinggi Djermania.
'There was nothing as lofty as Germany.'

Malahan ada jang membela tindakan Presiden itu dengan dalil "keadaan darurat".
'Then there are those who defend the President's behavior with the argument of "emergency".'

Sebenarnja ada suatu pertentangan perasaan dari dalam jang sukar mengatasi.
'In truth there is a conflict of opinion from within which it is difficult to surmount.'

At the beginning of sentences, particularly at the beginning of stories, ada occurs with the enclitic -lah which marks the predicate as standing at the beginning of the sentence.

Adalah seorang anak muda jang bernama Salam.
'Once upon a time there was a young boy named Salam.'

The order noun-construct, ada also occurs on occasion.

Taring tidak ada.
'There are no tusks.'

Tapi adik-adik tak ada jang mau tinggal.
'But there were no children who wanted to stay behind.'

4.2.4.2 In the second minor sentence type the verb ada is associated with an unmarked sentence structure that is a sentence structure which has neither a conjunction nor a connective preposed. The standard order is ada, sentence structure. Since unmarked sentence structures function syntactically as nominal structures, this sentence type can be considered to be directly parallel to that described in the preceding section except for the matter of word order; ada never follows the sentence structure as a whole, though it may occur between the subject and the verb.

The use and meaning of this type of sentence are discussed in different ways by different grammarians. On the whole it may be assumed to specify that the circumstances referred to by the unmarked sentence structure exist (or existed or will exist).

Ada orangnja menunggui.
'It happened that its people were guarding it.'

Sungguhpun ada djuga ia memakan buah-buahan.
'Indeed, it also happens that it eats different kinds of fruit.'

Sekali-sekali ada ia dipelihara orang didalam kurungan.
'It happens every so often that people keep it in a cage.'

Tidak ada satu Weltanschauung dapat mendjadi kenjataan, mendjadi realiteit, djika tidak dengan perdjoangan.
'It does not happen that a philosophical outlook can become an actuality, can become a reality, if there is no struggle.'

Sometimes _ada_ follows the subject of the unmarked sentence structure.

Sekali-sekali kampret itu ada menangkap kumbang.
'From time to time it happens that the bat catches bumblebees.'

4.2.4.3 The third type of minor sentence is one in which the verb _ada_ occurs with two nominal constructs, one of which precedes it, while the other follows. This order is fixed. Again it is difficult to decide on the precise relationship of the noun constructs to the verb _ada_. One possible interpretation is that the preceding noun construct is the subject, and the following noun construct is some sort of dependency; again, this dependency cannot be considered as the object of a transitive verb because there is no corresponding passive structure. The alternative possibility is to regard _ada_ and the following noun construct as forming a subject-predicate sentence in inverse order, as described in the preceding sections. In this case, the preceding nominal structure must be regarded as a topic; however, this topic is not linked to its comment by the enclitic -_nja_ postposed to the subject; this is characteristic of topic-comment sentences. It is probably best to regard it as a subject-predicate structure, the predicate consisting of the predicative _ada_ and its dependency.

If this interpretation is accepted, the meaning of this sentence structure is that the referent of the subject has, or is in possession of (_ada_), the referent of the object. Alternatively, if the other interpretation is accepted, the meaning of the sentence is that the referent of the subject exists (_ada_) as far as the referent of the topic is concerned.

This construction is sometimes contrasted with one utilizing the verb root _punja_. Thus, _saja ada rumah_ is said to mean 'I have a house at my disposal, though I do not necessarily own it', whereas saja punja rumah means 'I own a house, but I do not necessarily have it immediately available for my use'. This distinction would seem, however, to be a purely artificial one for most speakers, and can not be insisted upon. Both of these usages are rather colloquial; they find their way only occasionally into standard formal Indonesian in which 'I have a house' is rendered by saja mempunjai rumah.

Perbandingan itu ada benarnja.
'This comparison has validity.'

4.2.4.4 The fourth minor sentence type is that which has no subject, but only a predicate, even when it is a stimulus sentence. Such sentences refer chiefly to the weather, and the list of predicates is therefore considerably restricted. Examples of sentences of this type are

Hudjan.	'It is raining.'
Sudah malam.	'It is already dark.'

Diluar dingin.
'It is cold outside.'

Di Djakarta begitu panas.
'In Djakarta it is so hot.'

4.3 Interrogative Mode

Interrogative sentences in Indonesian can be directly derived from corresponding declarative sentences in the following ways.

4.3.1 Yes-no Questions

The interrogative sentence has the same form as the declarative sentence except for the intonation. In general, the pitch of the voice rises at the end of the question and falls at the end of the statement. The exact nature of the rise, its relative position, and its relative height are all matters which may vary depending on dialect or on the specific effect desired for the question. This difference in intonation is signalled in the orthography by the use of the question mark, and this is the only apparent difference between the two types of sentence.

Such interrogative sentences are of the type which expect either an affirmative or a negative answer.

Responses to questions expecting an affirmative or negative answer are given by using either ia, (sometimes ja or je) or, more formally, saja for the affirmation, and tidak, belum or bukan for the negation. These words are used to affirm or negate the validity of the declarative statement underlying the question. Their relationship to affirmative and negative questions is to be noted.

Siti pulang?	'Did Siti go home?'
Ia.	'Yes, she did.' '(It is true that Siti went home.)'
Tidak.	'No, she didn't.' '(It is not true that Siti went home.)'
Belum.	'No, not yet.' '(It is not yet true that Siti went home.)'
Siti tidak pulang?	'Didn't Siti go home?'
Ia.	'No, she didn't.' '(It is true that Siti did not go home.)'
Tidak.	'Yes, she did.' '(It is not true that Siti did not go home.)'

Another possible device is the repetition of that part of the predicate which will best serve to give the desired answer.

Siti pulang?	'Has Siti gone home?'
Pulang.	'Yes, she has.'
Belum.	'No, not yet.'

Sudah tua hamilnja?
'(Is the pregnancy already old?)'
'How far along is she?'

Boleh saja berbitjara sebentar?
'May I speak to you for a moment?'

Kau mengira perusahaan transport-ku hasil dulu itu?
'You are thinking that that old trucking business of mine was a success?'

Aku? Membantu dalam soal begitu?
'Me? Help in a thing like that?'

4.3.2 Interrogative-word Questions

Questions which require specific information rather than a simple affirmative or negative answer are formed by substituting an interrogative form for a particular item in the declarative sentence. The original order of the items in the declarative sentence usually remains unchanged; the interrogative form may, however, occur at the beginning of the sentence instead, for emphasis; this shift is especially frequent with the adverbial interrogatives.

It has been stated earlier what the interrogative forms are, but it will be well to list them here together.

apa?	Non-personal nouns, either as head of a nominal expansion or as a noun modifier in such an expansion. The nominal expansion may be governed

	by a preposition as in _buat apa_?, _dengan apa_?, etc.
siapa?	Personal nouns, under similar conditions.
mana?	Adjectives and any nominalization introduced by _jang_; usually with _jang_ preposed, but _jang_ may not occur if another _jang_ follows. Also colloquial for _dimana_?
berapa?	Numeratives.
dimana?	Locational adverbs denoting rest.
kemana?	Locational adverbs denoting motion towards a place.
dari mana?	Locational adverbs denoting motion from a place.
bilamana?	Adverbs of Point of Time.
apabila?	Adverbs of Point of Time.
kapan?	Adverbs of Point of Time.
berapa lama?	Adverbs of Duration of Time.
bagaimana?	Adverbs of Manner.
mengapa?	Adverbs of Reason or Cause.
kenapa?	Adverbs of Reason or Cause.

Mengapa is also on occasion used as a verb and is then the interrogative form for verbs; it is rare, however, that a question is so framed that an interrogative form for verbs is necessary.

Engkau mau apa, mas Noto?
'What do you want, Noto?'

Lalu pindahnja ke Djakarta bagaimana?
'Then how did you come to move to Djakarta?'

Pada siapa ia akan tinggal di Djakarta?
'Who would he stay with in Djakarta?'

Untuk apa engkau mau bertemu dengan aku?
'For what reason do you want to talk to me?'

Mengapa malam begini dan mentjuri-tjuri?
'Why at night like this, like a thief?'

Mana jang kita pilih, saudara-saudara?
'Which shall we choose, ladies and gentlemen?'

Dimana kalong tidur siang hari?
'Where does the flying fox sleep during the day?'

Dengan sendjata-sendjata apa sadja binatang-binatang jang sudah kita bitjarakan itu membela dirinja?
'With what sort of weapons do the animals which we have been discussing defend themselves?'

Bagaimana kita dapat membedakan kalong dan burung?
'How can we distinguish flying foxes and birds?'

4.3.3 Interrogative Markers

Declarative sentences can also be made interrogative by the introduction of one of the interrogative markers, apa and -kah, as well as a combination of these two, apakah.

4.3.3.1 The interrogative marker apa, which should not be confused with the interrogative non-personal noun apa?, occurs at the beginning of a sentence and the remainder of the sentence follows in standard declarative order.

Apa njonja kira saja tak dapat membesarkan anak saja sendiri?

'Do you think I am not able to raise my child by myself?'

Apa ia telah mempunjai radio-station, jang menjundul keangkasa?
'Did it already have a radio-station which butted against the sky?'

Apa Sulaiman tak akan meneruskan peladjarannja?
'Isn't Sulaiman going to continue his studies?'

Apa kau kira-kira mau membantuku djuga kali ini?
'Do you reckon you want to help me this time too?'

The possibility of ambiguity between the interrogative marker apa and the interrogative noun apa? 'what' is usually lessened in the following ways.

The use of the marker apa is colloquial, while the use of the marker -kah is both colloquial and formal. In most cases, unless the material is conversational, the use of the marker apa is avoided.

When the material is such that the marker apa does occur, it is always in initial position in its sentence; the occurrence of the interrogative apa? in this position in its sentence is therefore avoided.

When the interrogative noun does occur at the beginning of the sentence, some authors distinguish the two forms by adding the enclitic interrogative marker -kah to the interrogative noun, but not to the interrogative marker. Thus, apakah is always to be construed as the noun. But other authors make no such distinction and in their writings apakah may be either the noun or simply a redundant interrogative marker.

In the special case where apa? would be the object of an active verb, and, for reasons of emphasis, it occurs at the beginning of the sentence, certain other structural changes may also occur in the sentence. The verb is made passive and is nominalized by preposing jang. The original subject of the sentence becomes the agent in the passive construction, and is normally proclitic to it, and therefore inseparable from it; the passive verb then necessarily occurs without the prefix di-. Thus, the sentence

Saudara mentjari apa?
'What are you looking for?'

can be transformed so as to bring apa at the beginning of the sentence, and thus emphasize it, by arranging the items as follows:

Apa jang saudara tjari?
'What is it you are looking for?'

This sort of arrangement reduces the possibility that apa in the initial position will be construed as the interrogative marker instead of as the interrogative noun.

But here again, the marker -kah usually occurs.

Apakah jang saudara tjari?
'What is it you are looking for?'

4.3.3.2 The interrogative enclitic -kah may be postposed to any free word in the sentence. Naturally, it occurs with that item of the sentence which is of greatest importance in the question. Since the item of greatest importance in an Indonesian sentence usually occurs at the beginning, the enclitic -kah usually occurs with the first word, or one of the first words, in the sentence. If -kah is postposed to the predicate, however, the shifting of the predicate to the beginning of the sentence is avoided in cases where a recognition of the division point between the subject and the predicate might be rendered difficult.

Pentjurikah itu kiranja?
'Is it a thief, do you think?'

Samakah isinja?
'Is the content of it the same?'

Dapatkah kamu menerangkan peribahasa dibawah ini?
'Can you explain these proverbs below?'

Tahukah kamu sebabnja?
'Do you know the reason?'

Pada masa Lenin mendirikan Negara Sovjet adakah rakjat Sovjet sudah tjerdas?
'At the time when Lenin was establishing the Soviet State, was there a Soviet people which was already educated?'

Demikian gemarkah engkau akan musik?
'Are you as fond of music as that?'

Mau djugakah engkau memeliharakan anak itu?
'Do you too want to raise this young one?'

Tidakkah pula Hitler dimikian?
'Again, was not Hitler of the same sort?'

Bukankah nenek belum dewasa waktu itu?
'But wasn't it the case that you weren't yet a grown woman at that time, grandmother?'

Sudah pernahkah kamu melihat sepasang kera-peliharaan jang mempunjai anak ketjil?
'Have you ever seen a pair of tame monkeys which have a little baby?'

Even if there is another interrogative form in the sentence, -kah may also occur, and, in this case, it is postposed to that interrogative form.

Bagaimanakah giginja?
'What kind of teeth does it have?'

Binatang manakah menghasilkan "wool"?
'Which animals provide wool?'

Gerak apakah itu?
'What movement is that?'

Apabilakah angga rusa itu "kotor" tampaknja?
'When are the antlers of the deer apparently "dirty"?'

Tetapi kapankah Hitler mulai menjediakan diapunja "Weltanschauung" itu?
'But when did Hitler begin to develop this philosophical outlook of his?'

Apakah tjara jang berkeadaban itu?
'What is this polite manner?'

Apakah "Weltanschauung" kita, djikalau kita hendak mendirikan Indonesian jang merdeka?
'What is our philosophical outlook if we want to build a free Indonesia?'

Apakah permintaan Paduka tuan Ketua jang mulia?
'What is this request of the chairman?'

Apakah jang dinamakan merdeka?
'What is this thing called "freedom"?'

Apakah jang kita maksud dengan perkataan itu?
'What is it we intend with this question?'

Apakah jang harus kita buat untuk mengurangi bahaja itu?
'What is it that we must do to decrease this danger?'

4.3.3.3 The postposing of -kah to the interrogative marker apa produces the form apakah, which functions in the same way as the marker apa alone; some authors, however, as noted above, avoid this, and the form apakah in their works is always and only the interrogative noun and -kah.

Apakah maksud kita begitu? Sudah tentu tidak!
'Is such our intention? Far from it!'

Apakah kita hendak mendirikan Indonesia Merdeka untuk sesuatu orang, untuk sesuatu golongan?
'Do we want to build a free Indonesia for a certain person, for a certain class?'

Apakah tiap-tiap orang Rusia pada waktu Lenin mendirikan Sovjet Rusia Merdeka telah dapat membatja dan menulis?
'Was every person in Russia, at the time when Lenin was building a Free Soviet Russia, already able to read and to write?'

4.3.4 Confirmation Questions

A question in which the questioner merely expects a confirmation of his opinion is formed by means of a statement of that opinion in declarative form and with declarative intonation, followed by bukan, which, in speech, is usually separated from the declarative part of the sentence by pause, and which has itself an interrogative intonation pattern. In writing, it is usually marked off by a comma and the sentence end is marked with a question mark. Bukan may also be inserted parenthetically into the declarative sentence structure.

Pangkat mantri polisi amat tinggi pada zaman itu, bukan, nenek?
'The rank of Director of Police was a rather high one at that time, wasn't it, grandmother?'

Engkau tahu, bukan, bahwa pidjetan itu bisa merusakkan rahimmu?
'You know, don't you, that that massaging can damage her uterus?'

4.3.5 Choice Questions

A question in which the questioner is pressing for a yes-or-no choice is formed by putting the question in the interrogative affirmative followed by tidak, atau tidak, apa tidak, and so on.

On occasion, atau bukan may occur, particularly if the question is an equational sentence.

Betulkah demikian atau tidak?
'Is it accurate like that or is it not?'

Mau merdeka apa tidak?
'Do you want to be free or not?'

Tahukah kamu sebabnja maka tidak?
'Do you know the reason or not?'

4.3.6 Indirect Questions

Question structures can occur as nominal constructs in other sentences, thus forming subordinate clauses. They occur most frequently as the object of verbs and are not marked by any conjunction or by any change of internal order, but only by the interrogative markers which occur when they are independent sentences.

memisahkan mana jang salah dan mana jang benar.
'to distinguish what was false and what was true.'

Kita belum mengetahui siapa lawan siapa kawan.
'We did not yet know who was friend and who was foe.'

Saja tanjakan pada mereka apakah ini tindakan coup atau bukan.
'I asked them whether they had carried out a coup or not.'

Kita dapat menundjukkan dimana "kesatuan-kesatuan" disitu.
'We can point to where these "units" are located there.'

Question structures also occur as subjects.

Siapa jang hilang haknja atas tanah, hilang kemerdekaannja.
'Whoever has lost his right to the land has lost his freedom.'

Sometimes they occur as nominal structures in apposition to a pronoun subject.

Siapa jang membatja Pembukaan itu dengan teliti, ia dapat menangkap tiga buah pernjataan jang penting didalamnja.
'Whoever reads that Preamble carefully can comprehend three important declarations in it.'

4.4 Imperative Mode

Sentences in the imperative mode are derivable from sentences in the declarative mode. However, declarative sentences of the equational type have no corresponding imperative form. Declarative sentences which are passive likewise have no imperative form unless the imperative sentence is introduced by the negative imperative marker djangan.

4.4.1 In the imperative mode, the order and the structures remain the same as in the declarative, with the following exceptions. The subject of imperative sentences, with certain minor exceptions, is a second person subject, and may or may not occur in the sentence structure; more usually, it does not occur. The verb retains the same form as in the declarative sentence except that any transitive verbs in the active lose the prefix meN-; it is particularly to be noted that intransitive verbs which have the prefix meN- retain it in the imperative. A certain number of imperative markers are optionally used to mark the imperative. The negative imperative sentence uses the negative imperative marker djangan, rather than any such declarative negative modifiers as tidak, belum or bukan.

The enclitic -lah is frequently postposed to the imperative verb, since the predicate is in the non-standard position at the beginning of the sentence, and it becomes desirable to mark it as having predicate function. It is sometimes stated, however, that the use of -lah with the imperative not merely marks the predicate, but also softens the assertiveness of the command, and renders it less abrupt.

Batja sadja.
'Go ahead. Read it.'

Ini brandyku minum dulu, biar tahan lama!
'Drink this brandy of mine first, so that you can keep going!'

Ah, saja belum berani kawin, tunggu dulu gadjih f. 500.
'Ah! I am not yet ready to marry; wait until my salary is 500 florins first.'

"Sehatkan dulu bangsa kita, baru kemudian merdeka."
'"Cure first the ills of our people, and then be free."'

Membungkuklah, kubisikkan.
'Lean down! I'll whisper it.'

Lihatlah bodohnja harimau itu!
'Look at the stupidity of that tiger!'

Ingatlah akan hal ini!
'Remember this fact!'

Bandingkanlah kemerdekaan negara-negara itu satu sama lain!
'Compare the freedom of these states one with the

other!'

Terimalah prinsip nomor 3, prinsip mufakat.
'Accept principle number three, the principle of discussion.'

Perhatikan djugalah andjing jang mengedjar ajam.
'Be watchful also of the dog which chases chickens.'

Berdjoanglah terus sampai di achir djaman.
'Keep on fighting till the end of the world.'

Mendaratlah sebelum matahari terbit.
'Land before the sun rises.'

Batjalah buku itu.
'Read that book.'

4.4.2 The first class of imperative markers, tolong, tjoba, and silahkan, usually occur before the imperative verb form. If any of these markers is used, the enclitic -lah, if it occurs, will be postposed to the marker.

The marker tjoba, which is connected with the verb mentjoba 'to try', is a simple imperative marker with no further connotations.

The marker tolong, which is connected with the verb menolong 'to help', is used as an imperative marker in cases where the speaker desires that the action shall be performed for his benefit.

The marker silahkan, which is associated with the verb menjilahkan 'to invite', is used when the speaker wishes to indicate that the action is to be performed for the benefit of or as an accomodation to the performer; it conveys a definite connotation of politeness.

Tjobalah pikirkan hal ini dengan memperbandingkannja dengan manusia.

'Try to think out this question by comparing it with man.'

Masuk sadjalah kedalam dan tjobalah lihat.
'Just go in and see.'

Tolong bersihkan kamar saja.
'Help me clean my room.'

Silahkan duduk!
'Please sit down!'

Tjoba kita lihat apa dia masih hidup.
'Let us see if he is still alive.'

4.4.3 The second class of imperative marker includes the forms mari and ajo. These markers imply a request for cooperation, and the subject, when it occurs, is in the first person. If the subject is plural, as it more usually is, it is the inclusive first person plural pronoun. The subject occurs after the imperative marker. The enclitic -lah, when it occurs, is postposed to the imperative marker, and not to the following verb. The verb form is imperative, that is, transitive verbs occur without the prefix meN-, and passive forms do not occur.

Mari kita hadapi soal itu dengan tenang.
'Let us face the problem calmly.'

Ajo kita pertahankan negara kita ini.
'Let us defend this country of ours.'

Marilah kita bekerdja sehebat-hebatnja.
'Let us work as hard as possible.'

Mari saja uraikan apa jang dinamakan bangsa itu.
'Let me explain what is meant by a nation.'

4.4.4 The remaining imperative marker is the negative djangan. It occurs before the verb, which may be either active or passive, and which, if active, will retain the prefix meN- even in the transitive form. If the subject occurs, it precedes or follows the negative marker djangan. If -lah occurs, it is postposed to djangan.

Djangan membeli buku itu.
'Don't buy that book.'

Djangan dibatja buku itu.
'That book is not to be read.'

Kamu djangan membatja buku itu.
'Don't you read that book.'

Sekali-kali djangan diganggu.
'Do not be the least bit disturbed.'

Djangan mengira bahwa dengan berdirinja negara Indonesia Merdeka itu perdjoangan kita telah berachir.
'You must not think that with the setting up of this free Indonesia our struggle will be at an end.'

Akan tetapi harus kita djaga djuga, djangan hendaknja harimau itu habis punah.
'But we must also take care; it is desirable that the tiger should not become extinct.'

Djanganlah pembatja mentjari dalam buku ini falsafah sosial atau sematjamnja.
'Let the reader not seek in this book a social philosophy or anything of that kind.'

Djanganlah tuan-tuan gentar didalam hati, djanganlah mengingat bahwa ini dan itu lebih dulu harus selesai dengan djelimet, dan kalau sudah selesai, baru kita dapat merdeka.
'Do not be fearful of heart; do not think that this and that must be completed to the last detail, and when it is finished, only then will we be able to be free.'

Djangan terlalu banjak diberi nasi.
'Too much rice must not be given.'

Tiap-tiap djenis binatang hendaknja tjukup djumlahnja, djangan berlebih, djangan pula berkurang.
'Every kind of animal should be sufficient in numbers; there should not be an excess, and again there should not be a dearth.'

4.5 Exclamatory Mode

Sentences in the exclamatory mode may have the same form as sentences in the declarative, interrogative or imperative modes. Some of these may be partial sentences. They are, however, spoken with special intonational patterns; these patterns are usually represented in the orthography by the exclamation point at the end of the sentence.

Other sentences in the exclamatory mode consist of interjections, or of interjections followed by sentences in other modes.

Maaf, beribu maaf!
'Pardon, a thousand pardons!'

Merdeka Sekarang!
'Freedom now!'

O nduk, bukan main baunja!
'Oh, my dear, what a smell!'

Ajuh, bedebah, pergilah engkau!
'Oh! Woe is me! Go away!'

Ajo minggat!
'Let's run!'

Aduh, aduh, aduuuuh!
'Ouch, ouch, ouch!'

The following type of exclamatory sentence has its own particular structure. It is based on a declarative sentence in which the predicate is an adjective. The exclamatory sentence is introduced by the marker <u>alangkah</u>. The adjective forming the predicate of the declarative sentence follows, and the enclitic -nja customarily occurs with it. The subject of the declarative sentence follows.

Saudi Arabia merdeka.
'Saudi Arabia is free.'

Alangkah merdekanja Saudi Arabia!
'How free Saudi Arabia is!'

Revolusi kita progresif.
'Our revolution is progressive.'

Alangkah progresifnja revolusi kita!
'How progressive our revolution is!'

Alangkah hebatnja!
'How tremendous it is!

Alangkah lutju!
'How funny!'

Alangkah berbédanja isi itu!
'How different is the content!'

Alangkah berlainannja tuan-tuan punja semangat,--djikalau tuan-tuan demikian--, dengan semangat pemuda-pemuda kita jang 2 miljun banjaknja.
'How different are the opinions you hold--if you are as I described--from the opinions of our youth, two million in number.'

4.6 Complex Sentences

A simple sentence can be made complex by the introduction of one or more subordinate sentence structures as components. Sentence structures which are subordinated in this way to another sentence have specific markers to indicate the type of subordination. These markers are the conjunctions, and their function is discussed, and examples are given, in Section 3.6.2.

Three types of subordination are possible. A sentence structure can be made to function as a noun, to function as a noun modifier, or to function as an adverb.

4.6.1 Nominal Subordinate Clauses

Sentence structures which function as nouns may be either declarative or interrogative.

4.6.1.1 The declarative sentences are introduced by the conjunction bahwa. This conjunction is optional if the subordinate sentence is functioning as the object of a verb. It is, however, required if the subordinate sentence functions as the subject.

4.6.1.2 Interrogative sentences customarily function nominally as the object of specific verbs such as menanjakan 'to ask'. No conjunction marks such a clause, but the presence of the specific verb before it, and the presence of an interrogative marker in the clause, usually at its beginning, make the relationship abundantly clear. These are discussed, and examples are given, in Section 4.3.6.

4.6.1.3 Another subordinate sentence structure which functions as a nominal or as a nominal modifier is introduced by the conjunction jang. This conjunction is different from all other conjunctions in Indonesian in that it has a structural function in the clause in which it occurs; jang must always serve as the subject or topic of the clause which it introduces.

4.6.2 Adverbial Subordinate Clauses

Subordinate sentence structures which function as adverbs are introduced by a number of different conjunctions, depending on the meaning and the type of adverb which they happen to represent. Subordinate adverbial clauses occur in the same relative positions in the overall sentence structure as adverbs, with the possible exception that they occur less frequently between subject and predicate, or within the predicate, than adverbs do, unless set off by pause in speech, and by punctuation in writing.

4.7 Topic-comment Sentences

Topic-comment sentences consist of a topic and a comment. The topic is a nominal construct. The comment is a subject-predicate sentence structure of any type, mode or voice.

The subject of the comment is characterized by the proclitic -nja. Since the possessive pronominal enclitic for the third person has the form -nja, it would seem that the enclitic on the subject of the comment is this possessive enclitic. However, the enclitic for the subject of the comment remains -nja even when the topic is not in the third person, and this argues against an interpretation that this -nja is merely a pronominal form.

In effect, a topic-comment statement announces, in the topic, something about which a remark is to be made, and the comment supplies the remark.

Topic-comment sentences are more common in colloquial than in formal Indonesian. Perhaps contemporary Indonesian writers are rather strongly influenced by Western European languages in which topic-comment sentences are much less common at the formal level, except perhaps in French. This type of sentence, however, is commonly found in many languages of East Asia.

(The topic is underlined in the Indonesian examples only. In most cases, the translation does not attempt to reproduce a topic-comment structure since these are unusual in English.)

Rase atau Dedes, badannja sangat menjerupai badan luak.
'The rase or dedes, its body very much resembles the body of the civet cat.'

(Samakah isinja,) samakah deradjatnja negara-negara jang merdeka itu?
'Is the content the same? Is the degree (of freedom) the same in these states which are free?'

Karena apakah maka tikus itu banjak sekali ruginja bagi manusia?
'Why is rat damage very considerable for man?'

(Apakah jang dinamakan bangsa?) Apakah sjaratnja bangsa?
'What is called "a country"? What are the requisites for a country?'

Apa gunanja itu?
'What is the use of this?'

Geraham lipat itu gunanja untuk memamah makanan lumat-lumat.
'This complex molar's use is for chewing food extremely fine.'

Kebanjakan warnanja kelabu atau kuning-merah.
'The color of the majority of them is grey or tawny.'

Penjakit pes itu ada dua bentuknja.
'There are two forms of the plague.'

Manusia tidak djuga bisa dibekukan otaknja oleh propaganda.
'The brains of man cannot simply be frozen by propaganda.'

4.7.1 *Jang* as Topic

As has been mentioned, *jang* must function either as the subject or the topic of the clause it introduces. The following are examples of its occurrence as the topic.

djenazah kawannja jang dipindahkan makamnja
'the corpse of his friend whose grave was being transferred'

Kadang-kadang kita melihat kera jang pendek ekornja.
'From time to time we see a monkey whose tail is short.'

Apakah kita mau Indonesia Merdeka, jang kaum kapitalnja meradjalela, ataukah jang semua rakjatnja sedjahtera?
'Do we want a free Indonesia whose capitalists will rule, or one all of whose people are prosperous?'

"Minum!" kata teman-teman sambil membawakan sloki jang whiskynja telah mereka taburi abu sigaret biar tambah keras.
'"Drink!" said his friends as they brought him shots, the whiskey of which had previously been laced with cigarette ash so that it would be additionally strong.'

On occasion, anomalously, the enclitic occurs not with the subject of the comment, but with the object.

Kita mendirikan negara Indonesia, jang kita semua harus mendukungnja.
'We are building an Indonesian nation which we must all bear the burden of.'

4.8 Response Sentences

Response sentences are partial sentences which

depend on previous sentences to supply the key to their entire structure. Since the parts of the structure which are not repeated are omitted to avoid repetitiveness, there is no standard pattern which can be stated for the formation of such sentences except that those parts which do occur must be such as are compatible with a stimulus sentence structure.

An endless variety of examples could be adduced; only a few are given, since there is no underlying pattern to the manner in which response sentences relate to stimulus sentences.

Mendirikan negara Indonesia Merdeka jang namanja sadja Indonesia Merdeka?
'To establish a Free Indonesia which is a Free Indonesia in name only?'
(The preceding question begins Apakah kita hendak mendirikan... 'Do we want to establish...')

Di Sumatra biasa dinamai Mawas, di Kalimantan Majas.
'In Sumatra it is usually called mawas, in Borneo majas.'
(The subject orang hutan 'orangutan' is omitted in the first part, while subject, adverbial and verb are omitted in the second part.)

Mengapa tidak besok sadja?
'Why not tomorrow?'
(It is clear from the preceding discussion that this represents Mengapa Maman tidak pergi ke rumah Njonja Tirta besok sadja? 'Why don't you go to Mrs. Tirta's house tomorrow instead?'

C O N C L U S I O N

This grammar is basically intended for those who wish to learn to read and understand contemporary Indonesian. It will also be of value to those who wish to write or speak Indonesian, even though it does not go beyond syntax into the areas of stylistics and semantics. Much more research will be necessary before clear descriptions of these two areas can be produced. Some brief observations, however, may prove useful.

A good writing style is best developed by extensive reading and close observation. Since conventions differ from one people to another, both in language and in taste, early attempts at a good written style must be largely imitative.

In a good speaking style, the relative loudness of the voice, the position and movement of the hands and of other parts of the body, the expression of the face, the distance between interlocutors, are all important factors, especially in Indonesian. These factors can also be learned by observation and imitation.

In the same way, an appreciation of the semantic categories of the language and an idea of the range of meanings of each particular word are best developed by constant observation of the contexts in which the words occur.

The dictionary is also extremely useful in this connection. Certain facts must, however, be kept in mind in using a dictionary, particularly a bilingual dictionary.

First, by no means all of the words in the older dictionaries are in current use today.

Second, not all of the words which could conceivably be composed from a given root by the addition of prefixes and suffixes are listed in the dictionary; such words may be in current use, or they may not; it is always best, in creating a word by analogy, to determine whether it is acceptable or not before using it.

Third, most dictionaries fail to supply adequate information about the syntactic properties of the word defined, and also, in the case of bilingual dictionaries, of the word or words defining it; this can lead to many errors if due care is not exercised.

Fourth, the range of meaning or a particular word in Indonesian will never correspond exactly to the range of meaning of a word in any other language, unless, perhaps, the words are technical scientific terms; it is therefore better to develop a sense of the semantic range of a word in terms of the contexts in which it occurs in its own language, rather than by any method of translation between languages.

For this reason the use of an all-Indonesian dictionary as soon as feasible is earnestly recommended.

B I B L I O G R A P H Y

GRAMMARS

(The grammars listed are those actually consulted. A more complete bibliography can be found in

Teeuw, A., with Emanuels, H. W., A Critical Survey of Studies on Malay and Bahasa Indonesia; Martinus Nijhoff, 's-Gravenhage; 1961.)

Amin Singgih, Peladjaran Bahasa-Indonesia untuk Bangsa Asing; Balai Pustaka, Djakarta; 1956.

Aulia-Salim, N., Indonesian Language (Bahasa Indonesia); Tintamas, Djakarta.

Croes, H. C., Duin, H. M. and Van Dijk, A., Bahasa Indonesia; J. B. Wolters, Djakarta-Groningen; 1955.

Emeis, M. G., Inleiding tot de Bahasa Indonesia; J. B. Wolters, Groningen, Djakarta; 1950.

Fokker, A. A., Beknopte Grammatica van de Bahasa Indonesia; J. B. Wolters, Groningen, Djakarta; 1950.

Fokker, A. A., Inleiding tot de Studie van de Indonesische Syntaxis; J. B. Wolters, Groningen, Djakarta; 1951.

Hilgers-Hesse, I., Indonesisch; E. J. Brill-Verlag GMBH, Cologne.

Kaehler, Hans, Grammatik der Bahasa Indonesia; Otto Harrassowitz, Wiesbaden; 1956.

Kwee, John B., Teach Yourself Indonesian; The English Universities Press, Ltd., London; 1965.

Lie, T. S., Introducing Indonesian; Angus and Robertson, Ltd., Sydney, Australia; 1965.

Oplt, M., Učebnice indonéštiny; Orientální Ústav Čsav Praha, Prague; 1955.

Oplt, M., Učebnice indoneštiny; Státní Pedagogické Nakladatelství, Prague; 1966.

Overvliet, R., Wij Leren Indonesisch; Noordhoff-Kolff N. V., Djakarta; 1952.

Pino, E., Bahasa Indonesia for English-Speaking Students (I & II); J. B. Wolters, Groningen; 1953-1954.

Rambitan, M. H., Bahasa Indonesia (I & II); Noordhoff-Kolff N. V., Djakarta; 1950

Schmidgal Tellings, Indonesian for Today, Part 1; Djakarta; 1957.

Teselkin, A. S. and Alieva, I. F., Indonezijskij Jazyk; Izdatel'stvo Vostočnoj Literatury, Moscow; 1960.

Van der Molen, S. and Cemach, H. P., An Elementary Textbook of the Indonesian Language, Adapted for the Use of English Speaking Students; W. van Hoeve, Ltd., The Hague, Bandung; 1952

Van Eeden, W. Kr., Beknopte Spraakkunst op de Bahasa Indonesia; Persatuan Tenaga, Djakarta; 1952.

Zainuddin, S., Dasar-dasar Tatabahasa Indonesia; Balai Pustaka, Djakarta; 1956.

TEXTS

These texts formed the basis for this description of the Indonesian language. The primary text is given first, and the subsequently investigated texts are then given in alphabetic order by authors.

Ed. Sinaga et al., Dokumen2 Bersedjarah dalam Revolusi Kita; Panitia Konperensi Mahasiswa Indonesia SE-A.S., Washington, D.C.; 1961.

Den Hoed, G. and Soendoro, M., Fauna Indonesia (I & II); Noordhoff-Kolff N. V., Djakarta; 1953-1954.

Djilas, Milovan (tr. Mochtar Lubis), Kelas Baru; Badan Penerbit Suara Indonesia Raya, Djakarta.

Hatta, M., Demokrasi Kita; Pandji Masjarakjat, Djakarta; 1960.

Kipling, R. (tr. Darwis glr. Dt. Maharadjolelo), Anak didikan rimba; Balai Pustaka, Djakarta; 1959.

Nugroho Notosusanto, Tiga Kota; Balai Pustaka, Djakarta; 1959.

Pasternak, B. (tr. Trisno Sumardjo), Dokter Zhivago; Penerbit Djambatan, Djakarta; 1960.

Zuber Usman, 20 Dongeng Anak-anak; Balai Pustaka, Djakarta; 1957.

www.ingramcontent.com/pod-product-compliance
Lightning Source LLC
La Vergne TN
LVHW090805070826

844660LV00022B/1088

* 9 7 8 0 8 7 8 4 0 3 6 2 2 *